THE SIX-FIGURE BREAKTHROUGH

The Ultimate Guide to Becoming Debt-Free, Reducing Expenses, Increasing Your Income, and Investing for Your Future through Passive Income!

JEFF SHANNON

PAGE PUBLISHING
Conneaut Lake, PA

First originally published by Page Publishing 2024

ISBN 979-8-89315-253-1 (pbk)
ISBN 979-8-89315-260-9 (digital)

To the memory of Luciana Delos Santos

CONTENTS

PREFACE

The loss of a family member hits harder than any other type of pain, especially if that person was a big part of your life. I want to dedicate this book to the memory of Luciana de los Santos. Although I first met her in 2014 when my wife and I got engaged, I already knew how much she impacted my wife. On our first date, my wife talked about her family and Lucy. This was the person who raised her and took care of her all her life. When my wife graduated high school, Lucy sold her house so she could put my wife through college. No matter what my wife did or was going through, Lucy always wanted to help and be involved.

After my wife and I were married, we had a beautiful son. My job required me to go overseas at the time, so we helped Lucy fly from the Philippines to the US to help my wife with our newborn son. Since then, she has been with us through all the best and worst times. We didn't always agree on certain things, but she always had the best intentions. Four years later, we were blessed with a daughter. Lucy told me once that because of her age, she believed she was still here on this earth because of the children. She said they kept her active and loved being a part of their lives. Since she was too old to play with them how they wanted her to, Lucy always tried to cook for them or help them in any way she could.

During times when I needed advice, she was there to provide it to me, and she did the same for my wife. I always tried to show my appreciation and love by showering her with hugs and kisses, which she tried very hard to escape (I was faster!). I wish I had the chance to tell her how much I miss and appreciate her for everything she did for us, but sadly, I will never have the chance. While away on a business trip and in the middle of writing this book, I called my wife to share my progress with her. When I picked up the phone, my wife's voice when she answered left me speechless. With a trembling voice, she asked me if I received the message she had just sent me. When I opened my messages, there weren't any words. Instead, it was a picture of the wake for Lucy.

The sadness I felt overwhelmed me, and the guilt of not being at my wife's side brought tears to my eyes. Our children knew she was gone but didn't understand what it meant. I dedicated this book to her to honor her memory and our love for her. She will never be forgotten.

Lucy,

Thank you for everything you have done for our family. I know I'm not able to tell you in person, but know that we love you with all our hearts. Our children cherish every moment with you and discuss how much they miss you. I know you are in a better place now, and the kids know you are watching over them. I wish I had more time with you, but at least I was blessed by having you in my life. You will always be missed, and you will always be loved.

Sincerely,
Jeff

SPECIAL THANKS TO MY FAMILY

To my wife, thank you for everything you have done for our family. I appreciate you and love you more than words could ever say. You were there with me through the most challenging moments of my life and with me through the best of them. No matter where life takes us, let's enjoy every moment together. I look forward to spending the rest of our lives together. I love you and will always be there for you. Let's enjoy the present and look forward to a fantastic future together!

To my children, being your father and watching you grow into the wonderful kids you are has given me more happiness than anything else in this world. I'm so proud of how amazing you both are! You are kind, gentle, intelligent, funny, compassionate, and you love to help others. I love spending time with you and playing with you both. I can't wait to see the adults you will become. Stay focused in school and try to learn as much as you can. You can achieve anything if you never give up on your dreams because there is always a way to reach them. Whether you are happy or sad, you will always be able to talk to me about it, and I will help you as much as possible. I will always be here for you, and I love you both very much!

To my sister, Kayla, I am both proud and amazed at what you have accomplished. You have overcome many obstacles in your life and achieved something very few people have. You have a fantastic husband and two beautiful children. We are both swamped but thank you for taking the time to talk to me. I miss you and look forward to seeing where your journey takes you! I love you!

To my brothers, Dakota and Brien. Dakota, congratulations on getting married! You and Lauren have been together for so long that I already considered her family. She is a fantastic person, and I know you both will enjoy an incredible life together. Thank you for being there when I needed someone to talk to. I have always appreciated your straightforwardness and your honesty. I can't wait to see the new life you and Lauren build together! I love you both! Brien, you were the youngest of us, and because of this, I missed a lot of your childhood because I was living on the other side of the US. For that I'm sorry. That limited our time together, but I don't think I love you any less! You have always impressed me with how intelligent and curious you are. I love being able to talk to you and learn about the things you enjoy doing. I miss our time together and can't wait to see you again. I hope you can learn from my mistakes as well as my successes. They say knowledge is power, but only if that knowledge is implemented. Learn from my mistakes and plan for what you want in life. You have a bright future ahead of you, and I know you will excel. I love you and hope to see you soon!

To my mom, thank you for always being there for me and helping me when I needed it the most. You have done so much for me; I don't know where to begin. I love you and appreciate everything you have done for our family. You helped me through the darkest times when I felt like there wasn't a reason to continue. You might not have known, but you saved me. That is something I will never forget. I have been able to turn my life around. I'm now devoted to giving my best for my children (just like you have done) and helping as many people as possible to live a better life. Thank you for everything you have done for me. You have inspired me throughout my life and helped build the foundation that made me who I am today. I'm proud to call myself your son. I love you!

To my dad, thank you for all the things you have taught me growing up. Many of the things I'm great at now started from what you taught me when I was younger. My favorite hobbies also come from the skills I learned from you. You taught me how to build, how to fix things, how to troubleshoot, how to take risks, and how to enjoy the things we have. Those skills have helped me throughout my life in various jobs and helped shape me into who I am today. Thank you for allowing me to take risks and to be myself. Our relationship hasn't always been perfect, but I have always loved you and wanted to make you proud. I am letting my kids take risks and will teach them some of the things you have taught me so that they will grow up confident and booming when they grow up. I love you!

To my stepdad, thank you for everything you have done for me. One of my best memories from my childhood was the lesson you taught me about the importance of keeping your word. I asked you if you wanted to play catch with the football after you got off work, and you told me we would. You left early that morning but ended up working until sunset. I was a kid and didn't understand how exhausting work can be, so when you got home and said it was getting too dark, I got upset (sorry for that). After you changed from your work clothes, you saw that I was upset and told me to get into the car, and you took me to the park where we played catch for I don't know how long. I know that playing catch isn't a big deal, but it impacted me in more ways than you know. In a world where words don't seem to matter, yours did. You kept your word to me, meant the world to me, and still do to this day. I love you and am thankful to have you in my life. I always keep my word and honor the lesson you taught me. One day, I can impact someone's life the way you did mine and continue to do. Thank you for everything. I love you!

INTRODUCTION

What you are about to read is a step-by-step process of how to get out of debt and begin your investing journey and the exact steps I took to change my life. Your decision to purchase this book was the first step in becoming financially free and living the life you want to live. It doesn't matter how young or old you are; it is never too late to start. My goal is to give you, my readers, all the steps necessary to get your finances in order. I will show you the following:

- How to get out of debt
- How to reduce your expenses
- How to build an emergency fund and debt management
- Ways you can increase your income (short-term and long-term)
- Advice on building your résumé and preparing for a job interview
- How to use credit cards correctly (and enjoy their rewards) and improve your credit score
- Start investing in the stock market with low risk for long-term growth
- Learn about other investment options you may not have heard of
- Start investing in real estate and living in your house for free while building passive income
- How to plan for and live the life you truly want to live

Your journey will ultimately have three phases, which are essential in achieving your ultimate goals. In the first phase of your trip, you will learn how to reduce your expenses while increasing your income. This combination is powerful because it allows you to have more cash flow available. You will use this cash flow to build an emergency fund that will protect you from unforeseen accidents or circumstances that will keep you from being put in a desperate situation. Once you have your emergency fund, you can now start focusing on paying off your debt. When used correctly, this cash flow will accelerate the rate you pay off your debts, utilizing one of the two methods mentioned in this book. Once debt-free, you will complete phase one of your journey and start phase two.

Phase two begins once you are debt-free, in which you will focus on utilizing your available cash flow to acquire the assets that will ultimately allow you to earn enough passive income to replace your current income and continue growing your investments. If you follow this book as written, you should have, at a minimum, doubled your income by this point, which will allow you to quickly start earning passive income. Eventually, you will get to the point where your monthly passive income equals your monthly expenses when you are essentially considered financially free. However, this isn't truly the case. Because of inflation and stock market fluctuations, your passive income must be much higher. Many people say that you want your passive income equal to or more than your expenses to become financially free. I'm afraid I have to disagree and recommend trying to get your passive income streams to at least double your costs at a minimum because science and technology have improved enough that we are living over ninety years old and with inflation, prices, and the cost of living continue to rise over time. If we have another major recession, the market could drop by 50 percent, and homes could lose 30 percent to 50 percent of their value. By having your passive income at least double your expenses, you will continue to thrive and grow your investments simultaneously. Suppose you also continue to invest during these times. In that case, your investments will grow at extraordinary amounts as prices return to normal and increase!

You are ready to enter phase three once your passive income equals double your expenses.

Phase three begins when your passive income is double your expenses and you want to continue increasing it so you can eventually have it equal to the income you earn from your primary job. By following the methods in this book, you should gain much more than you started. Once you can replace the income earned through your job with passive income, you no longer have to work if you choose to do so. If you decide to continue working, you will now earn twice the income from your job alone, allowing you to invest in even more assets that will continue to grow over time. You will now have the ability to create generational wealth to pass down to many generations. Suppose you teach your children how to be financially responsible and how to invest. In that case, they can continue building on the foundation you set for them.

Although there are thousands of other ways to increase your income, the methods listed in this book were the most reliable sources that are not only easy to do, but I have done most of them myself. Although I had a lot of job experiences in the past, all the methods used to become debt-free and increase my income were new skills that I acquired through research and taking action (which you will find in this book). So regardless of where you are in life, these methods can be used by anyone. I did my best to ensure I wrote at an easily understood level and in an easily applied manner. My intention was to make it simple enough to understand but thorough enough to allow them to be utilized correctly.

I will provide you with two primary investing methods (and a few other solid investment options) that are not only easy to do but also how most self-made millionaires became millionaires in the first place. To invest in these things, the income you earn from your job and the methods listed here will grow your investments until your passive income is where you want it to be. I recommend using both investing methods simultaneously, simplifying the process as much as possible so you can focus on other things.

My decision to write about improving your résumé was to help you climb the career ladder toward a better income. Many people need to gain the skills, experience, or qualifications to get a higher-paying job and feel stuck earning minimum wage. Many people don't know what to do to change or improve this part of their lives, and some don't want to. I will help you make a better résumé and show alternative education choices that can earn more annually than many associate and bachelor's degrees while being significantly cheaper and providing hands-on learning (great for those who don't like the typical classroom setting). Your education is essential, and taking these steps will open many new opportunities for you.

Time is the only thing you can never get back in this world, and managing your time is valuable. Your stock investments will be a long-term investment strategy that will continue to grow over time with the fantastic benefits of compounding interest. Your real estate investments will generate income immediately, allowing you to reinvest that income and acquire more assets over time. By growing both simultaneously, you will be able to retire early by earning more income passively than what you made through your job, and both of your investments will grow over time. You can then use the equity you built in your real estate investments as leverage to expand your portfolio without using your income to do so. Your assets will be earning income, which you can use to purchase more assets so that they continue to grow faster every month.

I can't promise the results you will get because it is up to you to take action. It is up to you to wake up every morning to do your best. However, I can promise that your life will improve if you put in the work and implement the things in this book. I know this because you will achieve things that you didn't think were possible for you before. Your mindset will change when you realize that every action you make today results in the future you will have tomorrow. You will succeed if you continually work toward your long-term goals with a plan to get there.

It's time to take the steps necessary to become the person you were meant to be. You can change every aspect of your life, and I hope this book helps you transform your life. This may be the hardest thing you have ever done, but it will also teach you more about yourself than anything else. You will have to set aside your doubt and rise to the challenge. From now on, don't tell yourself what you can't do or what you can't achieve. All you are doing is limiting the potential that's inside of you. It's time to break free of the chains holding you back and create your future. I want you to succeed, and I know you can do this. Now let's begin.

CHAPTER 1

IMPORTANCE OF UNDERSTANDING FINANCES

IMPORTANT STATISTICS TO KNOW

- Three in four Americans who earn less than $50,000 are living paycheck to paycheck, compared to roughly two in three of those making $50,000 to $100,000 (https://www.bankrate.com/finance/credit-cards/living-paycheck-to-paycheck-statistics/).
- Most Americans have $1,000 or less in personal savings in 2023, a third have $500 or less saved, while 8.5% have between $501 and $1,000. Meanwhile a whopping 11.4% said they have no savings, the survey found (https://www.nasdaq.com/articles/most-americans-have-$1000-or-less-in-savings-how-to-increase-that-amount).
- US income by gender: The median male salary in 2022 was $52,612. The median female salary was $39,688 (https://www.fool.com/the-ascent/research/average-us-income/#:~:text=U.S.%20income%20by%20gender%3A%20The,income%20in%202022%2C%20at%20%24101%2C027).

When you look at these numbers, it seems absurd to think that most of the United States is financially irresponsible, but this is our world.

We now live in a time when debt is considered normal, and if you can't afford something, you can use a credit card and make monthly payments. The chances are that almost every person you know is in debt and won't have enough to retire on. This is a significant problem that we face that isn't being talked about and an issue that is continuing to grow.

Financial literacy is so critical because it can make the most significant impact on your life. Financial struggle is one of the leading causes of divorce and one of the most important contributors to stress that most people face. If you could eliminate all debt in the world right now, I guarantee that within the first year, more than half of the world would again be in debt. The problem isn't the debt itself but how we manage our finances.

I want you to look at the statistics I mentioned at the beginning of this chapter and see if this is where you're at now. After you finish reading this book and apply the methods, you will no longer be one of those statistics. Effectively managing your income will make a significant difference in your life. I'm not only going to show you how to manage it but how to grow it. Your purchase of this book tells me you are tired of living paycheck to paycheck and drowning in debt. Use those feelings to motivate you. Use the pain holding you back to drive you toward success.

LIVING ABOVE YOUR MEANS

One of the most significant reasons we are experiencing this problem is because the majority of the United States is living above their means, trying to live a lifestyle they can't afford, and spending money they don't have. They end up accumulating debt until their expenses are higher per month than their income. This is the perfect book for you if you are currently in this situation. Not only will it help get you out of that situation, but it will help you to be able to live the lifestyle you want to live.

People spend so much of their time and money trying to impress others. Instead of wasting your time trying to impress people who don't know or care about you, I want you to focus on improving your life so you can afford the things you want. You might be thinking that you aren't able to escape your current situation or that you are destined for a life of poverty, but that isn't true. It doesn't matter where you start but the path you decide to take. You must determine whether you want to continue living a life of debt and stress or take the steps necessary to obtain financial freedom for yourself and your family.

When I first lived on my own at the age of seventeen, I was making minimum wage. It took me five years to be considered middle class. Unfortunately, the more money I made, the more I spent. The other problem it gave me was getting approved for credit cards with absolutely no idea how to use them. For thirteen years, I accumulated over $100,000 in debt. I was living above my means, spending more money than I should, driving a car I couldn't afford, and living in a house I shouldn't have been living in.

Sadly, this is what is happening to most people in the middle class. In the lower class, most of their income goes toward expenses, with whatever else is left going toward liabilities. The middle class tends to increase their costs in proportion to their income but spends a lot more on liabilities (such as new vehicles, RVs, expensive electronics, and vacation homes). The upper class tries to keep their expenses as low as possible while using most of their income to purchase assets that will earn them money. They then reinvest that money into things that will make them passive income and use the income earned to reinvest back into more assets. They also leverage debt strategically, benefiting massively from the results. Something I found interesting is that many millionaires purchase vehicles that are several years old (after five years, a vehicle loses around 70 percent of its value). They pay in cash, so they aren't losing money toward interest.

Regardless of which class you are currently in, you need to reduce your expenses and stop living above your means. You need to increase your income and invest in assets that will eventually provide passive income for the rest of your life. If you follow everything listed in this book, you will have everything you need to start doing this with the best methods I have found. Doing so will allow you to be in control of your life and accomplish the things that you have once considered impossible.

I spent thirteen years struggling and accumulating debt before learning what would make a difference. I ended thirteen years of struggle within a year and a half of hard work and sound financial practice. The best time for you to start is now. There is no reason for you to continue living a life filled with stress and pain. Learn from my failures so you don't make the same mistakes. If you are currently in this situation, you must acknowledge that you made mistakes and that your choices got you there. Once you can admit this, it will feel like a weight has been lifted off your chest. You know you made mistakes, and now you know you must complete the necessary changes to correct them.

Some people won't understand that you're trying to change your life for the better, and others may try to purposely keep you from doing so. Some might even try to make you feel guilty for wanting to escape your current situation and make something of yourself. If you have a lot of negative people in your life, it might be time to let them go. It is essential to surround yourself with people who want to see you succeed and people who will support you. Find successful people and try to learn from them. Continue to grow your knowledge and start networking with different types of people. Mindset is everything, and the most significant difference between those who succeed and those who don't is how they think and what they believe in. They don't just take opportunities; they create new ones. If you are constantly trying to grow and learn, you will be able to overcome any obstacle you encounter.

How to utilize this book

The best way to use this book is to read entirely through it at least once but follow along and do these things in order because each thing leads to the next. This will give you a complete understanding of what you will be working toward so you know what to expect and prevent you from losing all your hard work and progress. After that, use the Contents to take you to the parts you need to refresh your memory. If you don't enjoy reading, I will include a "cheat sheet" at the back of the book that will give you the information in bullet points in its simplest form. I hope that by adding this the people who don't enjoy reading can go to the back of the book to understand the basic concepts and then go to the pages that go into more depth if further clarification is needed. I will also include a list of tips in the back of the book that can save you hundreds of thousands of dollars throughout your lifetime.

It took a lot of time, research, and experience for me to be able to write this book. Thank you for your purchase and for trusting me to provide this information. If this book helps you change your life, tell others you know about it so it can also change theirs. Continue following these steps for the rest of your life. You will not only be highly successful, but you will also be able to pass on your legacy to your children.

I look forward to hearing about your success and the changes this has made to your lives, so please leave a review and let me know where you are on your financial journey.

Thank you!

CHAPTER 2

CREATING YOUR PERSONAL FINANCIAL STATEMENT

What you are about to read will be one of the most excellent tools to get out of debt and start your journey to success! Initially, it will help you manage your debt and keep your expenses low. Once debt-free, you can continue using this tool to plan for a fantastic future. It will take longer the first time you do this, but after a while, it should only take you a few minutes. The following information is crucial for your success, and I encourage you to do these things as you read this book! After you create your first one, please make sure you save it. It will be a great motivator when you can look back and see how much progress you have made, even after only a few months.

What you are about to create is a simplified version of a financial statement (essentially a combination of an income statement and balance sheet for your personal use), so it will appear a lot different than what you would see when comparing it to the financial reports of a business. It may be simple, but it's all you need and perfect for those doing this for the first time. So without any more delay, let's get started!

To create your first personal financial statement, you will need a pen or pencil and two sheets of paper (if you want to make a digital copy, you can do so later once you finish setting it up). With the first sheet, I want you to divide it into four quadrants (divide the paper into four equal parts). Now we are going to label the top of each section.

In the upper-left section, I want you to write "Monthly Income," and in the upper-right section, I want you to write "Monthly Expenses." In the lower-left section, I want you to write "Assets," and in the lower-left section, I want you to write "Liabilities."

It should look like this once you are finished:

Monthly Income	Monthly Expenses
Assets	Liabilities

You should set it up this way because it makes it easier to explain and understand. The items on the left side of the page (your monthly income and assets) are the things you want more of. The things on the right side (your monthly expenses and liabilities) are the things you want to eliminate or decrease.

Once you set up the different sections, it's time to fill in the boxes. Please note that once you better understand how this works, you can make your own however you like. If you do, just be sure you have the same information! Unfortunately, the left side will be almost empty for most people starting out, and that's okay! We all start from different places; what truly matters is that we try to get where we want to be.

If you are married or consider getting married, make sure that you and your partner are on the same page financially! This is very important because you need to work together to make this work. If you aren't on the same level, it will not only cause problems but also hinder you from making progress! You are a team and need to work together to succeed. If both of you work toward the same goal, you will get there faster and have a stronger relationship. Talk to your partner about the journey you are about to make, and make sure they want to make it with you. This will significantly improve your communication because you are solving problems together. Even if you become frustrated with your partner during this process, do not yell, talk down to them, or be condescending. They are trying to help you, and you need to appreciate them for their hard work. If you do have a disagreement, don't start accusing them. Instead, ask them about what happened and try to work it out. Be respectful and compromise. You got this!

FILLING OUT THE INCOME SECTION

Unfortunately, the expense section will be the most extensive for most people. That is okay because in the next chapter, we will go through them and eliminate or reduce as many as we can. If your income stays the same but you lower your expenses, more cash flow will be available. Suppose you need help remembering all the ones you have. In that case, apps like TrueBill can help you identify things you are paying monthly and possibly forgot (Planet Fitness membership?).

Items to include in the Expenses section are the following:

- Rent/mortgage payments
- Water/electric/gas/phone/internet/medical bills
- HOA/condo fees
- Car loan payments
- Auto/home/renter's/landlord/health/life insurance
- Transportation cost (gas for vehicle, bus, taxi, shuttle, Uber, etc.)
- Credit card payments
- Loan payments (personal loans, auto, consolidation, etc.)
- Child support
- Groceries
- Fast food and restaurants (keep separate from groceries)
- Netflix/Disney/Hulu (any streaming service)

- Grooming and clothing
- Entertainment (date night, out with friends, etc.)
- Gym memberships/competitive sports
- Other

This list has the things that came to mind, but many things still need to be included. If you spend money on something, add it to the list. Later on, you can shorten the list to include certain categories. Hence, it is easier to manage, but we want to identify all expenses for now.

FILLING OUT THE ASSET SECTION

This section may be small for now, but once your debt is paid off, you will start investing in assets that grow in value and earn income. It is perfectly fine if you don't recognize some of these things I wrote. List your current assets. Later on, you will be investing in many different investments.

Items to include in the Asset section are the following:

- Real estate
- Stocks
- Bonds
- REITS
- MLPs
- Funds
- CDs
- Business or business ventures

Again, this list doesn't include all assets. This is just something for you to get started with. Later, when we discuss emergency funds, you will add your emergency fund to the asset list. If you have any assets that I haven't mentioned, please list them.

FILLING OUT THE LIABILITIES SECTION

Items to include in the Liabilities section are the following:

- Mortgages
- Student loans
- Auto loans
- Personal loans
- Credit cards
- Essentially anything that you owe a balance on

If you owe money to a friend or family member, list it under Liabilities because you will need to pay them back. And if you do, make sure to thank them for helping you out when you needed it.

FINISHING UP THE PERSONAL FINANCIAL STATEMENT

Once finished, write "Total: ______" at the bottom of each section. Add up your income and enter the amount in the appropriate part. Do this with each section and double-check your math to ensure you made no mistakes. You can add "Cash Flow" to your personal financial statement if you want to track that (cash flow = income - expenses). Now that you have finished filling in all the sections, you will use the other sheet of paper to organize everything. Create the same quadrants on your other sheet of paper, followed by the name of each section. Afterward, list the name of each item on your new sheet from highest to lowest numeric value (each section should be organized from the highest value to lowest), but don't put the numbers just yet. Once you place the names in the correct order, you can make twelve copies of your paper (so you won't have to recreate the list each month) and then go back to your sheet and fill in the numbers. The last step is to date the top with the current date.

I recommend either posting your first one on your wall or framing it. As you start making progress, you can look back at where you started, and it will motivate you to keep pushing. Learn from your past mistakes and let it serve as a reminder. For more motivation, you can create your vision board with your goals and dreams to visually see where you are in your journey. If this interests you, go to YouTube and watch videos on how to make one. It could be an excellent time for you (and your partner) to think about and make long-term plans for your future!

You may have noticed that real estate is listed as a liability and asset, which may be confusing, so I will clarify. Under Liability, you would list the price that is owed on the mortgage, and under, you would list the value of the property if you were to sell it today (if you made a $20,000 down payment on a $100,000 home, you would list $80,000 under Liabilities and $100,000 under assets [$100,000 - $20,000 = $80,000]).

The first time I created my personal financial statement, I was shocked and highly concerned. My income was less than my expenses, meaning I was spending more money than I had every single month. This is a terrible position, but it was the sign I needed to let me know I had to do *everything* it took to get out of debt. If you are scared or worried about your current situation, see that it will improve if you implement the steps in this book. Now, you have the tools and knowledge necessary to get through this. Keep reading because it will definitely change your life!

Now that you know where your money is going every month, we can identify the problems and plan to go forward. It may take a while the first time you do this, but the next time, it should only take a few minutes. While there are software/apps that can help you do it digitally, I recommend starting this way in the beginning. There is a budgeting app called Mint that is very good, and I recommend considering it. Doing it on paper is a great way to start, but feel free to use an app if you are more comfortable with it.

In the next chapter, I will discuss budgeting and reducing expenses. You want to lower your costs before you focus on increasing your income. Most people fail to make progress because the more they earn, the more they spend. We can reduce your expenses by half, and then I will discuss ways to increase your income. I hope you are ready because the following two chapters will use your personal financial statement as a tool to change your life. This is where it starts to get exciting! If what you have learned already has helped you, please leave a review on Amazon. It helps me and will make this book more visible to others so they can improve their lives as well!

CHAPTER 3

BUDGETING AND REDUCING EXPENSES

Now it's time to put all that work you did in chapter 2 into action! This chapter aims to help you reduce your expenses to give you more cash flow. These are changes that can be made immediately and can make a significant impact on your current situation. Before we start, there is one thing I want to reiterate. *If you are married or intend to get married, you and your partner have to be on the same page!*

As I mentioned earlier in this book, financial stress is one of the most significant contributors to divorce. My wife and I are partners in life and work together in everything we do. Now our communication is fantastic, and instead of arguing about finances, we discuss the best ways to invest our income for long-term financial gain. Instead of arguing, we work together and compromise. This is what I want for you. I want you and your partner to work together and learn to communicate. Identify problems together. Solve problems together. Plan your future together.

As you go through this book, some things here can be stressful because it is new and different. The last thing you want is to be going through that while your partner thinks you are wasting time, making it even harder for you to deal with. Work through this together and work on the game plan together. By doing so, you will get out of debt and increase your income faster than doing it alone!

ELIMINATING AND REDUCING EXPENSES

Now that I have made it clear you need to be on the same page if you have a partner, I want you to take the personal financial statement you made and lay it out in front of you. If you have one, I want you (and your partner) to go through your expenses and see what you can reduce or eliminate altogether. Examples could be streaming services like Netflix, unused gym memberships, eating at fast-food/restaurants, etc. The goal is to figure out what you can immediately reduce now (once you are debt-free, feel free to add some of these things back if you need to).

You don't have to go the extreme route like I did. I eliminated and reduced everything I could because I'm the type of person motivated by results. I knew the process would be complicated, so the more effort I put into it, the faster I would be out of the situation. You might not want to remove your streaming service, which is fine. This is your journey to make. I want to give you as much information as I can that will help you the most. You decide what to do with it.

QUESTIONS YOU NEED TO ASK

Once you have gone through the list and decided what you can eliminate and what you can reduce, I want to provide a list of questions for you to ask yourself. After you consider the question, I want you to pick up your phone or drive to the location and take action. These questions can have a significant impact on your expenses and liabilities, so please address all them. The worst that can happen is the person on the other line can say "no." In the worst-case scenario, your situation won't change much. In the best and most likely scenario, you can significantly reduce your monthly expenses and liabilities.

These are the questions I want you to ask and take action on:

- What internet package do you have, and are you willing to get a cheaper one?

- What phone plan do you have? Are there cheaper options available?
- How much is your grocery bill, and will you change your dietary habits to reduce it?
- If you are renting, how much is your rent, and can you move somewhere cheaper once your lease is up?
- What do you pay for auto insurance, and can you get a lower price? (You will have an emergency fund later on, so a higher deductible will get you a lower monthly payment.)
- How much are you paying for health insurance, and is there a better, more affordable plan? (When you have an emergency fund, a higher deductible will result in lower payments.)
- Do you use public transportation and/or taxis, and if so, is the transit close enough for you to walk or ride a bike?
- How long have you had your auto loan, and can you refinance for a lower monthly payment?
- If you have a mortgage, can you refinance your home for a lower monthly payment?
- Do you have student loan debt, and if so, have you attempted to renegotiate payment terms with the lender?
- Suppose you need help paying the minimum payments on your credit cards and/or loans. Have you contacted your bank to see if they have a "hardship" program to significantly reduce your interest rates (usually down to 0–3 percent)? If they don't have a specific program, they can still negotiate your current rates with you.
- Have you considered debt consolidation on high-interest rate loans and/or credit cards to make managing the payments more manageable and possibly have a lower-interest rate? (You only want to do this if it lowers your overall interest rate.)
- For your electric bill, have you called to see if they charge more during a particular time of day or if they have a program or system to help reduce your monthly bill? (Most companies do.)

- For your water bill, can you hand wash dishes to save water, change from baths to showers (reduce the time spent showering), or use settings on your washing machine and dishwasher to use less water?
- If you have medical bills, have you gone to the hospital/clinic and spoken to their financial aid department, or have you gone on Google and typed the words "financial aid" followed by the name of the hospital/clinic?

Depending on your income, you could have a certain percentage up to the entire amount of the medical bill waived. If you don't meet the requirements to reduce your bill, you can still negotiate a lower monthly payment (some people get it down to $20 a month!).

As you can see, there are many ways to immediately reduce your expenses and liabilities, and most people don't think of these things. When I started my journey of becoming debt-free, it never occurred to me that these were options. If you haven't done so already, review all these questions again and call the appropriate location to see what changes you can make. When you call them, try to have the current information available and write down the new information on a blank sheet of paper. The goal is to compare later to see the overall cash flow you will have available after reducing your expenses.

When I did this, I could refinance both of my vehicles and reduce my monthly expenses toward auto loan payments by $223. The city I lived in charged more for electricity used during midday, so we only ran the AC at night and opened windows and used fans during the day (we were hardly home during the day, so this saved us a lot), which dropped our electric bill by $120 a month. Debt consolidation on two cards reduced my monthly bill by only $60. Still I had a lower-interest rate and made only one monthly payment instead of two. Refinancing two vehicles, changing how we used electricity, and consolidating debt reduced our monthly expenses by $403. These weren't the only things we reduced but just an example of the difference these things can make!

STEPS TO TAKE NOW!

Today and tomorrow, go to your bank and speak to someone to see if they can help with the things I have mentioned. Call other locations and see what you can have reduced. Even if you can only mitigate a couple things, it will make a big difference in your available cash flow and give you (and your partner) more breathing room and a better foundation to stand on. To summarize this chapter, reduce your expenses *as much as you can*! The more cash flow you have, the faster you will become debt-free! Every month, you will create a new personal financial statement, so each month, I want you to compare where you are now and where you started. You will feel motivated and inspired to keep making progress. In the "Other" section under the Monthly Expenses section, make sure you give yourself a small allowance to reward yourself occasionally (even if you only give yourself $100). You are working hard, so treating yourself (and your partner) once or twice a month can motivate you to keep going!

In the next chapter, I will discuss different ways to increase your income immediately and provide information to increase your income over time. Even if you don't decide to utilize the information in chapter 5, you can still get out of debt by simply reducing your expenses and applying your available cash flow toward paying off your debt. However, before you begin paying off your debt, you must have an emergency fund (which is covered in chapter 4). I have these chapters in a particular order because everything builds off the previous steps.

CHAPTER 4

EMERGENCY FUND AND DEBT MANAGEMENT

EMERGENCY FUND

This may be one of the shortest chapters but also one of the more important ones. If you implemented the steps from the previous chapter, you should have been able to increase your available cash flow. In chapter 5, I discuss ways to increase your income immediately and in the long-term. I also advise writing résumés, preparing for job interviews, and choosing a career path that will allow you even more opportunities in the future. This is to give you a path to earning a higher income as you go through life.

Before you skip ahead, you need to understand the things in this chapter because this is the one that matters the most. This chapter will provide you a safety net to prevent you from ending up in the same situation in the future and provide the exact methods to pay off your debts. We'll talk about the importance of an emergency fund, how immense it should be, what it should be, and what to do after you have it.

An emergency fund sounds like funds that should be used for emergencies only. Many financial experts recommend having anywhere from three to six months of your expenses saved as an emergency fund. However, I believe three months isn't enough. If you lost your job today without any notice, you would have to update your résumé and start applying for jobs. The response rate for job applications is low, so using one hundred jobs might result in less than ten responses back and only two to three opportunities to set up an interview. After your initial interview, some jobs require a second interview. Once you get hired, you must complete all the paperwork, and the company has to submit it, which takes two to three weeks on average. Depending on how long it took for you to get the job in the first place, you could have already spent one and a half to two months to get to this point. Once you start working, you may not get your first paycheck on time, depending on your hiring date, HR, and the final date for that particular pay period. In the best-case scenario, the earliest you are looking to get your first check is at least three to four weeks for most people (possibly two weeks if your job pays weekly).

You might think, *But that is still within three months, so that should be fine…*; it depends on the scenario. Emergencies are unpredictable, and just the example I gave happens more often than you realize. Nothing wrong can occur from having more than enough. Still if you don't have enough to cover the emergency, that is when the situation starts to look dark. I recommend having *six* months' worth of your expenses in your emergency fund. So take the personal financial statement you made earlier and look at your monthly expenses. Take that number and multiply by 6. This is how much you need to save for your emergency fund.

Hopefully, you have been following the steps I have provided, and you already reduced your monthly expenses by a significant amount. If not, I would like for you to do so now. Remember, this is for your future, not mine. I have already been through this process and understand its importance. On your personal financial statement, go to your Asset section and write "Emergency fund: ___ out of _____." Your calculated emergency fund amount will go in the second blank space you made, and the amount you have saved up for it will go in the first blank space (if six months of expenses came out to $12,000 and you have $600, this is how it should look like: "Emergency fund: $600 out of $12,000). As you contribute to your emergency fund, you want to update your personal financial statement each month. Hence, you know how much you need left.

Contribute to your emergency fund until you reach your goal, and make sure your emergency fund is in a yield savings or checking account that you can readily access if an emergency happens. The purpose of a high-yield checking or savings account is to help prevent you from losing your emergency fund through inflation. Regular checking and savings accounts give you less than 1 percent interest while inflation averages around 3 percent per year. Money left in a checking/savings account will slowly lose value over time. How long it takes depends on how much you need to save and how much positive cash flow you have available. You have already reduced your expenses, and the next chapter covers ways to increase your income, so utilizing the things within this book will be the fastest way to get out of debt.

DEBT MANAGEMENT

From this point forward, your goal is to make sure you make all minimum payments on time. I don't want you to miss another payment in the future. Your job now is to take your cash flow and start adding it to your emergency fund *before* you start paying off your debts. This keeps you on track if an emergency happens and you can't afford to take care of it. This prevents you from being put in a desperate situation where you feel like you must use a credit card. We are done with that. Until you are debt-free, you shouldn't be using a credit card. I will provide an entire chapter devoted to proper credit card usage, improving your credit score, and how to earn money using a credit card and enjoy the rewards they can bring. Until you are debt-free, please don't use them.

Once you have saved up enough to cover your emergency fund, you can use two popular methods to get out of debt. The first is the *avalanche* method, and the second is the *snowball* method. I have tried both, and the snowball was the best one for me. The avalanche method focuses on paying off the debts with the highest interest rates first. In contrast, the debt snowball method focuses on paying off the smaller amount first. You will put your available cash flow into whatever debt you are paying off. Once you pay it off, you will take your cash flow (plus the amount you were paying monthly on the debt you just paid off) and start paying on the next one (if my cash flow was $500 and I just paid off a loan that was $50 a month, I would start paying $550 extra, including what you were paying as a minimum payment, on the next debt). The more debt you pay off, the more cash you have available to pay off other debts.

The one that will make you debt-free the fastest is the avalanche method because paying off the higher-interest rates first will save you more money in the long run. I prefer the snowball method, and the reason it is the most recommended by financial experts is that by paying off the smallest amount first, you can see your debt going away, and it is visually motivating. Most people find the snowball method to be the best. Still I recommend you watch different YouTube videos on the topic. People are more likely to continue doing it if they can see it working, which is why it works best for most people. You decide which method is best for you. I'm someone who is motivated by results.

You will start to see that using your cash flow and the payments you made on paid-off debts will significantly change your debt situation and expenses. You will also notice that with a few paid off, you don't need to have as big of an emergency fund as you had before. I have two recommendations, but your choice will be based on your preferences.

The first method (and the one I would do) is to take the additional funds not needed in your emergency fund and use it to pay off your debt. A big payment would significantly speed up the process. Also if you receive a tax return, add it to your emergency fund if it isn't finished or use it to pay off debts. Any additional income you receive should be used to pay off debts.

The second method is the same regarding receiving a tax return. Still the difference is I want you to take the additional funds no longer needed for your emergency fund and use them to treat yourself (and your partner if you have one). Take the time to relax and give yourself (and your partner) a much-needed break. While I believe it is best to get out of debt as soon as possible, you must ensure you and your family aren't being neglected because of it. You don't have to use all of it, but take some time for yourself and your partner. If you want, you can save it to be utilized later.

Ultimately, you can do whatever you want. I aim to give you all the tools you need to succeed. The next chapter provides many ways to speed up the process by increasing income. You can more than triple the income you are currently receiving. No matter how much your income increases, always try to keep your expenses low and try not to acquire any liabilities. The secret to becoming wealthy isn't in making money but the ability to keep it and have your money work for you.

CHAPTER 5

BUDGETING AND INCREASING INCOME

This is my favorite chapter as it makes the most significant difference for my family and me. In chapter 3, I went over reducing your expenses and the various ways to do so. Unfortunately, you will always have costs, so you can only reduce them to a certain point. Income, however, has no limit. I only realized how easy it was to make money once I started seeing opportunities I never recognized and creating new ones as I increased my knowledge. Much of this has to do with your mindset, but when I struggled daily, my brain was on autopilot, just trying to get by. It wasn't until I invested much of my time into reading books that I realized I was looking at everything from the wrong perspective.

Instead of thinking *I don't make enough money*, I began to ask myself, "How can I make more?" It was a simple switch but one that changed my life forever. I would credit this change in mindset to the book *Rich Dad, Poor Dad* by Robert Kiyosaki. When it came to working at my job, instead of thinking about all the negative things, I began to see it as an opportunity and a challenge to overcome.

How you view the world and your perception of things affect your mindset. The most significant limitations you could ever face are the ones you place on yourself. You never will if you keep telling yourself you can't do something. You have opportunities all around you to improve your life, and even if the doors of opportunity are open, you will never see them with a closed mind. Stop telling your-self what you can't do or can't accomplish in the future. The person reading this today is different than you were before you bought this book because you decided to invest your time learning how to change your life. Now you have the information needed to do so. It's up to you to put these things into action. *No more excuses!* A job is simply a tool to get you where you want to be. Use the available tools and resources and make them work for you.

ASK FOR A RAISE

The first and easiest thing you can do is ask for a raise at your current job (unless you just started or have been underperforming). Obviously, you want to do it in person and schedule a time with your boss (depending on your job type) to sit down and discuss it. How you ask can make a big difference, so before you ask, you should prepare. You want to create a sales pitch about why you should get a raise to help convince your boss. Your boss generally has a lot of responsibilities and may need to be made aware of everything you do for the company.

Have you successfully solved problems that the company was experiencing? What is the average pay for your position in the area, and are you making less? Are you doing the work of multiple people? Are you always on time and reliable and come in to cover for others? Is your overall performance consistently higher?

Put together a sales pitch that answers those questions, and then approach your boss during the scheduled time. The most crucial part is that regardless of whether they approve or decline your request for a raise, *stay polite and professional.* Don't let the actions of others dictate your response. If they say no, ask what changes you could make or what you could do that would qualify you for a raise. There can be many reasons they said no, and it might not have anything to do with you, so don't take it personally. Never be afraid to ask questions, and never be scared of rejection. You only lose when you decide to give up or never try at all.

SECOND JOB

While this idea may not appeal to you initially, a second job could provide a steady stream of reliable income. This is important because the more income you generate, the faster you can get out of debt and the more you will have to invest. Whether you decide to get a second job as a short-term or long-term plan, know that your primary goal is to *get out of debt*! If your primary job offers overtime, try to get as much as possible (I will talk more about overtime in the next paragraph). If your primary job requires a lot of physical work, try to get a second job that requires little physical work so you aren't pushing yourself too hard. If your primary job doesn't have a lot of physical requirements but is mentally exhausting, get a secondary job that requires little mental effort. The best second job is one that works with your schedule the most.

OPPORTUNITIES FOR OVERTIME

Another thing to consider is if your job has opportunities for overtime. Most overtime will pay time and a half, so it is an excellent way to earn more income; 26.7 hours of overtime is equivalent to forty hours with your regular pay. If you have a job offering overtime, try to get as much as possible. If it doesn't, I would recommend looking for jobs that do. Not all jobs provide it, but if you are willing to do the work, you can easily double your check for less work than a second job would give you. During the journey to financial freedom, I worked multiple jobs to accelerate debt repayment. At one point, I approached my supervisor at my main job to inquire about overtime opportunities. The company was short-staffed, and they were eager to have additional help, so I was offered ample overtime hours. This allowed me to resign from one of my secondary jobs and focus on my primary job, which was the highest-paying among them.

My schedule became demanding, but after a few months, I transitioned to a more flexible option, like delivery driving for DoorDash, to prioritize my well-being and rest. Despite the fatigue, the goal of financial independence fueled my determination to continue.

Eventually, my dedication paid off. Not only did I eliminate my debts, but I also secured my dream job, which offered a significant increase in income compared to my previous jobs combined. Today, I'm thriving in this role, grateful for the journey that led me here.

HOUSE HACKING

This method is fantastic if you have a mortgage or rent an apartment/home and are allowed to sublease. Not only is it a great option, but it is essentially passive income once you get it set up. While I was working multiple jobs, my wife could not work because of the cost of childcare. We had a mortgage on our home, so my wife and I discussed the idea of optimizing our space by getting roommates and exploring Airbnb. Considering our property was in an area considered popular for tourist, our location seemed ideal for Airbnb rentals. However, since we were living in the house ourselves, we decided to rent out a room instead of the entire property. We listed our main bedroom on Airbnb as it offered a private bathroom, and we relocated to one of the smaller rooms.

While I was occupied with work, my spouse took charge of managing our house-hacking endeavors, demonstrating impressive skills and efficiency. Thanks to the strategies outlined in this chapter, my spouse was able to leverage our home to generate a consistent monthly income. Overall, our house-hacking efforts contributed significantly to our monthly income, thanks to the amazing efforts of my wife.

I want to share my appreciation and love for my wife. While I was fully occupied with multiple jobs, my wife took on the tremendous responsibility of managing our household, including caring for our children and overseeing the house hacking methods mentioned in this book. Managing a household, especially with children, is a significant task in itself. My wife's dedication and hard work played a crucial role in shaping who we are today. Our journey, through debt, strained our relationship, but instead of giving up, my wife stood by my side. Together we conquered our debts and are now focused on building a bright future for our family.

I've always been grateful for my wife's contributions, but I realized that I hadn't expressed my appreciation enough. When I learned that my partner didn't feel valued, I made sure to communicate my feelings. Now I want the world to know how much I admire and appreciate her.

My partner has been my rock, providing unwavering support and reminding me of our goals when I felt overwhelmed by work. Not only did she support me, but she also worked tirelessly to manage everything else. To my beautiful wife, I am deeply grateful for everything you do for our family, and I love you more than you could ever know!

HOUSE HACKING WITH AIRBNB

If you decide to do Airbnb, check with your area to ensure you are within the guidelines and follow all the rules. If you are renting, there may be other options than Airbnb. If that is the case, renting to roommates may be your best option if you are allowed to sublease.

To start with house hacking with Airbnb, figure out if your location is excellent for Airbnb (pretty much any tourist spot or amusement park is a given, but if you live close to a lovely beach or near a big college, you can also find good opportunities). If so, you want to list a bedroom that has a private bathroom. You want to furnish it with both new and nice furniture and a TV with a streaming service (we got a lot of five-star reviews for this reason!). Depending on the size of the room, add a mini fridge and fill it with a few bottled waters (it isn't required but definitely helps). Type up a list of things to do in the area or get the free brochures you can find in local stores that show all the tourist attractions in your area. Place those neatly in the Airbnb room. List a deposit on the room if something gets damaged, and Airbnb will ensure it gets paid back to you (Airbnb has fantastic customer service and responds quickly).

Always have two comforter sets (buy them specifically for Airbnb use and keep the receipts), so when the customer leaves, you have a clean set to prepare the room for the next guest while washing the other one. You also want multiple towels for your Airbnb guest (buy them specifically for Airbnb and keep the receipt). When you set up your page, make sure your house and property photos look amazing. Another thing to do is list a cleaning fee. Because you will frequently wash the comforters and towels, you will be using a lot of water and detergent, not to mention the cleaning products used to scrub and clean the toilet and shower. Vacuum and sweep every time a guest leaves so the room is spotless for the next guest. You want the rest of the house to be pristine as well.

If you are listing your place, list it below the average price to generate traffic and get reviews (great reviews earn you the SuperHost status). This will make your home one of the first to show up when people search your area. If you are only renting the room, make sure you don't leave that out (you don't want people thinking they are renting the entire place and then find out it's only a room; you will get negative reviews if that happens). Any time you buy cleaning supplies or furniture for Airbnb, save your receipts and provide them to your CPA when it's time for you to do your taxes (a lot of people think they're expensive, but they actually cost the same as places like Jackson Hewitt and H&R Block). This can be tax deductions for you!

Check your state laws to see how long someone can stay on your property before they are considered a resident. Airbnb will allow you to list short-term and long-term rentals (you can choose the maximum length they can stay). There have been stories where someone booked for a twenty-day stay in a state that considers them a resident if they stay longer than fourteen days, and the person refused to leave the property. After speaking to the police and a lawyer, the Airbnb host had to give the other person a thirty-day notice to vacate the property. Please ensure the length of time they can rent your place is less than the number of days determining residency to protect yourself. This is very rare, but I think it's good practice to plan ahead.

How to find roommates

When my wife and I considered getting roommates, we initially wanted to avoid the idea because we heard horror stories of people with roommates. After doing Airbnb, we realized it wasn't as bad as we imagined and was a pleasant experience. There are many websites to find roommates, and the ones we used were Roommates.com and Roomster.com (they both cost to use, so don't list until you are ready to start receiving messages from potential renters and only do one at a time). When we recorded the price, we made it "All utilities included," which made it easier because we didn't have to go through the hassle of dividing the utilities and arguing over the amount. It makes it easier for your roommates because they know what it will cost every month. They will pay significantly less than they would by getting an apartment and not having to worry about utilities.

The best way to list the price was to search for the average rent of a one-bedroom apartment in your area. If the room you're renting has a private bathroom, multiply the average one-BR price by .63 (if the average rent for a one-BR was $1,500 a month, you would list the room with a private bath for $945). If it will be a shared bathroom, multiply the average one-BR price by .56 (if the average rent for a one-BR was $1,500 a month, you would list the room with a shared bath for $840). The only exceptions are if the room is small or if the house is in poor condition. I would also recommend rounding (if the number you get is $747, do $750). If the room is tiny, you will have to lower it even more, but these are the prices that we found to be best (we started low and increased it until we found a higher and consistent number). The prices may seem high once you understand that including utilities is very fair for them.

If you list a room for rent and instantly receive many messages, you set your price below average. While this can be good for getting someone in the room faster, we usually find a solid roommate with a higher price within two weeks. Most of our roommates were terrific, and I decided to share my strategies with some of them so they could do the same thing with their own house one day! If the house is in poor condition, you must list the price lower until you can bring it up to a higher standard.

RENTING EXTRA ROOMS AS STORAGE

If you have extra rooms or a garage/shed that needs to be in use, you don't want roommates; you can earn extra income by renting out those spaces as personal storage using an app called Neighbor. If people don't have a lot of things to store, they will much rather pay half the price to keep their stuff in a small AC-controlled room (because it is controlled if the space is in your house and you can often list your space just slightly under the average price for a unit). If it is a bigger space like a garage, you can divide it up by marking the floor with tape or by building divider walls. Remember that you need to be available to allow people to come get their stuff, so you will set the times you are available. You would also want to be present when they get their things to ensure they don't touch anyone else's belongings. This makes less than the other options. However, it is still a decent way to increase your income using resources already at your disposal.

Some people buy sheds from Lowes and Home Depot to place in their yards and rent them out. Once they are paid off, they believe more and use the income from the other units to pay it off. To use this strategy, you will need a decent amount of space; depending on where you live, you may be required to get permits to have a shed. When you buy through Home Depot and Lowes, they do the process for you, but check with them before you decide to go this route.

USING YOUR VEHICLE TO GENERATE INCOME

The value of vehicles depreciates faster than any other purchase you will ever make. Vehicles tend to lose 10 to 30 percent of their value the day you drive them off the lot, and within five years, the value loses around 70 percent of its value. This means buying a used vehicle that is five years old will give you a car for 70 percent less, which is still usually covered by the warranty. One of the biggest mistakes people in the middle class make is purchasing a brand-new (and expensive) vehicle and driving it for a few years before deciding to trade it for another brand-new car. Now they not only owe twice as much as the vehicle is worth, but they also usually roll the negative equity into another brand-new vehicle that will lose 10 to 30 percent of value just from driving it off the lot.

Auto loan debt is one of the most significant contributors to debt and a big reason people are stuck in their current situation. If you look at the average spending and vehicles throughout the classes, it's shocking. You would think that millionaires would drive these flashy (and some of them do) nice cars. At the same time, the lower and middle classes went for reasonably priced vehicles.

What you quickly realize is that it's the opposite. Usually, the lower- and middle-class families purchase brand-new vehicles (and pay interest), and the upper class tends to buy used cars (in cash). The lower and middle classes tend to only consider how much the monthly payment will be instead of how much they will pay throughout the loan. The upper class cares more about cost efficiency and investing in assets that earn them money, so they prefer buying a used car that has already lost a decent amount of value and paid in cash so they aren't wasting money that can be invested by paying interest.

If you are like the majority of the United States, you have an auto loan with high monthly payments and interest. There are several methods I know of to generate income using your vehicle, so I will list them out and explain how to do them.

Uber/Uber Eats, DoorDash, Grubhub, Lyft

You may have heard of these or used their services to get to a particular destination or have food delivered. You may have even worked one of these as a side hustle. Before you rule them out, know that you can earn consistent and reliable income using them, and they deserve more than minimum wage a lot of time. It also gives you the flexibility to make your own schedule. Out of the ones mentioned, I have personally driven for Uber, Uber Eats, and DoorDash. My wife has driven for Uber, Uber Eats, DoorDash, and Grubhub.

My wife and I prefer DoorDash, Uber Eats, and Grubhub over the others for one simple reason. You don't have random strangers getting in and out of your vehicle; it comes with a feeling of safety. Uber and Lyft allow you to become a taxi, but you can't refuse people service. I am highly allergic to cats, but if a customer needs a ride, I accept, and if they happen to have a cat or be covered in cat hair, I still have to give them a ride. You aren't allowed to refuse a driver, and it's treated the same as discrimination. Uber Eats, DoorDash, and Grubhub will enable you to pick up someone's food order and deliver it to their homes. Often they have you leave it outside their door, so you don't even have to deal with the people at all. You can also listen to whatever music you want or have a phone conversation without bothering anyone. It is a low-stress job that is an excellent supplementation option.

To sign up for these, you obviously need a vehicle (in very crowded cities, you can use a bicycle) and provide proof of insurance and a driver's license. The food delivery services usually send you a bag to keep food warm and other accessories for you to use (like the DoorDash card and hand sanitizer). It can take anywhere from a few days to a few weeks.

Getting approved varies. DoorDash was the one both my wife and I were instantly approved for. Grubhub never approved mine or responded, but they accepted my wife's application within two weeks. The rest were all about a week on average. It depends on your area and which is more in demand, but you can do multiple simultaneously. My wife would cycle through them if the one she was currently using was slow. Even though Grubhub was more complicated to start because of the waiting period and the selection process, the pay was more than the others for the same amount of work (I believe my wife was averaging between $15 and $18 an hour from Grubhub, which was suitable for the area we lived in). However, with DoorDash, you could essentially drive any time you wanted. When I was doing DoorDash, it was between $12 and $15 an hour, which was suitable for my area.

Uber and Lyft are great options if you don't mind having random people in your vehicle. Where you live depends on how much you make, but you can make much more if you live close to an airport and a big city. My first Uber trip was from an airport to a city one hour away, and in my first hour of driving, I made $97 plus a $20 tip. If you live near an airport, I believe you will have the best chance at making much more than driving people around town. Even with the additional pay from Uber, I chose DoorDash as my go-to. Within six to eight hours, I typically make an extra $100. After quitting my second job (my main job allowed for overtime, so I didn't need it), DoorDash became the replacement for my second job because of the schedule flexibility (the perfect side hustle for reliable income).

If you work on a rotating shift and your schedule is hard to work with, DoorDash is your best option. Choosing your own schedule and being able to work at almost any time allows you to work no matter what you do. Are you a single parent? I know many people who use DoorDash and bring their kids with them. You only get out of the car to pick up food and drop it off. If you are a single parent struggling to find work because of the cost of childcare, I recommend going this route.

Paid advertisements on your vehicle

This one tends to be city-specific, but if you live in a decent-sized city, consider using your vehicle as an advertisement. There are a few that are reliable, but there are also scams, so be careful. The app I used was Wrapify (another reliable one is Carvertise, but unfortunately, it was not for my area at the time). You download the app and provide pictures of your vehicle and vehicle information. The app tracks your driving route for a few weeks up to a few months. This is done to determine the amount of visibility your vehicle would generate as you drive regularly. While doing this, my commute to work was almost an hour's transit, depending on traffic. Hence, it only took a few weeks to get an advertisement offer.

The first offer was for me to put this suction-cupped sign on top of my vehicle, and they would pay me $320 a month for a two-month contract. If I accepted (I did), they have you drive to a local shop. They will put it on your vehicle and make sure the GPS tracker is working, take a picture of it to send to the company, and that's it. All you do after that is drive like you usually do. After the first two months, I received another offer for a vinyl sticker for my back windshield. The pay was $120 a month for a three-month contract. I have yet to receive another offer after those two, but I got an extra $1,000 over five months of driving for free. The reason I didn't receive any more offers was likely due to the advertisements not generating enough income from the city I was in to make the ad cost worth it. Regardless, this is a simple way to earn extra income by doing nothing other than continuing your regular schedule.

APPS AND SIDE HUSTLES

The stuff I'm about to talk about now may require specific skills, but luckily, you can find something you are good at and make money for it. There are many apps to choose from that allow you to sell your services, and one of the better ones I found was the app called Handy. This app is perfect for those with a particular trade or skill; you can make a decent amount while doing this. My first example is someone I met who mounts TVs. That's literally all he does. It doesn't matter how big or small the TV is; he charges a flat rate of $80 (in the city I lived in, this would be the exact cost if you had the store come out and do it for you, but you could get someone through the app to do it a lot sooner).

When my wife and I decided to do Airbnb, we wanted the TV mounted so it took up less space, but I didn't have any of the tools to do it properly and didn't want to buy them for one-time use, so we used the app. The following day, the guy showed up at our house and had the bracket and TV mounted within thirty minutes. They were anchored correctly and level. After asking a few questions, he said he does it as a side job to supplement his income, and during the weekends, he is mounting anywhere from three to twelve TVs a day. He worked in a different city than he lived, so between the two, he always had work when he wanted it. He not only used the app to get jobs, but he also had business cards and would pay for advertising on social media.

Other similar apps include Task Rabbit. This one is similar but more general in the options to choose from. Handy was more geared to plumbing, electrical, tiling, and backsplashes. Task Rabbit had anything from "Ikea furniture assembly" to dog walking. By the way, assembling Ikea furniture in my area had prices listed for $17 an hour to $50 per item assembled. If this is something you like doing or are good at, it may be an excellent option!

OTHER CONSIDERATIONS FOR INCREASING YOUR INCOME

While the abovementioned things can increase your income immediately, I wanted to provide more information to increase your income permanently. These will be things that you need to consider and things that will require more thought and preparation.

The easiest way to increase your income for most people would be to consider moving to a location with higher pay. While this might sound obvious, many people never live one hundred miles outside of the city in which they were born. Don't believe me? Try going to your high school reunion and see how many people from your school still live in the same town or city. I bet several of them are still working at the same job they were working at when you graduated. It isn't necessarily bad, but it limits the opportunities available to you. Sometimes, it could be the fear and uncertainty of moving to a new location or a fear of starting over.

Regardless, please give it some thought. Maybe soon, it's a possibility for you. If you do decide to move, do it with a plan. Research the income (don't move without having a job secured) versus the cost of living. If the job is in a city, check locations outside the city (you can benefit from a lower cost of living that being outside the city offers while benefiting from the higher income that working in a city provides). Some companies pay you to relocate while others give you housing.

Suppose moving is an option for you and you don't have any marketable skills. In that case, you can apply to the military, Job Corps, shipyards, merchant marines, Peace Corps, Red Cross, etc. These are valid options that teach you a marketable trade or skill and provide solid career options and opportunities you never knew existed. Many of these will provide housing or a housing allowance, allowing you to get out of your situation and start a better life. It doesn't matter where you come from or how poor or broke you are; opportunities like these can be the things that will change your life forever.

I have a friend who is a deckhand for a company that works on merchant vessels who was straight out of high school with no experience. Yet he is making more money than the average American. Not only that, but he also loves his job, which has much growth potential, meaning he can move up in the company. I know several merchant marines make over $200,000 a year. One is an engineer with a bachelor's degree, the other worked his way up through the company and in a similar position.

If you want to talk about the military, it has the most potential to completely change your life. Any job you can get as a civilian, you can get in the military. They provide you a place to live, send you to schools you wouldn't otherwise have access to, and provide on-the-job training that is better than anything you can get outside of the military. The best jobs in the military for transitioning back into civilian life are jobs in the communications field, electronic technicians field (any technician-related job actually), and cybersecurity and IT-related fields. Many jobs can provide a six-figure income outside the military, especially if you have a security clearance. Imagine being in the military for four years with your living expenses paid for, receiving state-of-the-art training, leaving the military with free college tuition if you decide to attend or use it at trade schools or to go toward certifications and being able to immediately land a high-paying job. Want to buy a house? You can get one using a VA loan that doesn't require a down payment. If you feel there is no chance you will be able to change your life, I will be the first to tell you that you're wrong. You have countless opportunities; you must look for them and recognize them as they come.

CREATING A RÉSUMÉ (PREPARATION)

When it comes to writing a résumé, there are essential things that you need to know to have your résumé stand out above the rest. Consider your résumé as an advertisement to the company you are applying for to show them why you would be an asset. You are selling yourself, and you want your résumé to show your results and accomplishments with other companies because they want you to achieve similar results for them. Writing a résumé can feel challenging for many people, but it doesn't have to be. You can take steps to increase your chances of landing a great job.

The first thing that I recommend is creating a general résumé that you will use to write down all your skills, qualifications, experience, work history, accomplishments, certifications, and education information. This "résumé" isn't meant to be sent out but a collection of all your information so you can build "targeted" résumés for each individual company. This may take you a few hours but start by writing down your work history, your current and most recent being first. You want to establish a timeline of your work history, and you want it to be as complete as possible. If you have gaps where you are unemployed, note that on your "general" résumé, and we will return to it later.

Once you have your work history written down, list any achievements or accomplishments you have made for each job and write it next to it. What things did you do that saved the company time, made the process more efficient, solved a problem for the company, etc. For each job, try to list at least five accomplishments and achievements. When you write your targeted résumé for a specific company, you will reduce the amount listed and use the most relevant ones for that particular company.

Suppose you have a college degree or any certifications. In that case, you will list them under the education portion of your general résumé. You want to list the school, city, and state of the school, the dates you attended high school, college, or trade school, and/or the dates you obtained a degree or certification. You will do this for each one. If you are attending college but still need to complete your degree program, write down the same information as you did earlier, but list the credits you have obtained and the expected graduation date. You will need this information later on.

Suppose you have any skills with specific software, such as Microsoft Excel. In that case, you should list them in your résumé and your proficiency level (intermediate or expert). Fluency in multiple languages could also be considered a skill, so take note of that. Remember, this is for your "general" résumé, which you should treat as a rough draft. Typically, your skills/certifications will be one category and education will be another. However, not everyone will have some of these, so group them together now.

The part most people need help with is their profile summary. This is essentially your "elevator pitch." You should give a very brief summary of your résumé with just a few short lines. For your "general" résumé, try to write a line for each skill, certification, and experience you have listed so that when you register your "targeted" résumé, you can pick and choose the relevant lines to create your summary. For example, on one of my previous targeted résumés, my summary was the following: *"US Navy Submarine veteran with an advanced electronics education and engineering systems qualifications. Quality assurance craftsman skilled in building quality assurance packages, material handling, and project management. Cybersecurity student currently enrolled in a degree program."*

If you notice, I left out pronouns. I kept it simple while providing a good summary of my experience relevant to the position I was applying for. In my profile summary, the hiring recruiter will know I'm a military veteran with an advanced education in electronics and engineering systems. When they get to my résumé's skills/ certifications and education portion, they will find the actual schools completed and the certifications obtained. Being a veteran, they will also understand that I've had a lot of hands-on experience reflected in my accomplishments as they go through my work history. It also shows that I have experience writing QA (quality assurance) packages, material handling, and project management experience. While your profile summary should briefly summarize your résumé, mine is different for every résumé I prepare. Although I also have a fiber optics certification, it wasn't relevant for this particular job I applied for (I still had the certification listed on my résumé but left it out of my summary). The purpose of the summary is to provide a brief but clear and concise summary of what you bring to the table that is *relevant* to that particular company.

CREATING A RÉSUMÉ (PREPARING FOR A TARGETED RÉSUMÉ)

At this point, you have most of your personal information written down, so all the hard work is done. Now it's time to do a little research on companies you plan on applying for. Remember, you want to apply for jobs you're qualified for to have the best chance of success. Every job posting should have a job description with a list of requirements. Seventy-five percent of the résumés submitted for a position are written by people who don't meet the minimum requirements to get the job. Not only does it waste the time of the people going through résumés, but it also reflects poorly on you.

For larger companies, software is used to filter through résumés to automatically separate the ones that have what they are looking for and get rid of the ones that don't. Before your résumé is seen by a person, you need your résumé to get past the software, and you do this by going through the company's career page and looking at the job description. You want to look for any keywords that you notice as these are the types of things you want reflected in your résumé. You will tailor your résumé for each job by using this method. Use the language that is used by the company to increase the chance of your résumé being accepted for review.

My favorite website for job searching (and the one I've had the most success with) is Indeed.com, and I highly recommend you checking it out. If you want to work in the IT field, search for five different companies hiring in that particular field and go through the job descriptions and write down all the keywords you find. If you notice that many are using the same words and terminology, it needs to be in your résumé if it's applicable to you.

When I first started talking about résumé, I told you to create a general résumé for your personal use to build targeted résumés from. The website Indeed.com allows you to upload your résumé, and if hiring recruiters are looking for something specific that happens to be in your résumé, they will be informed and more than likely reach out. For this website, create a general résumé for that particular field (the five or six companies you searched for in the paragraph above) you are interested in and upload it. This will bring recruiters who are looking for someone like you directly to your inbox. For jobs that you apply for, you should submit a targeted résumé specifically for that company.

I went through this process and uploaded a résumé that used the keywords from several companies I was interested in, and within a few days, I began receiving messages from recruiters. Within two weeks, I had over fifty messages, which allowed me to have many options and negotiating power later on. Uploading a general résumé created for a specific type of job position or industry is a very powerful way to find a great job quickly.

CREATING A RÉSUMÉ (ORDER AND FORMATTING)

When you start your targeted résumé, you want to ensure all the essential categories are listed with your font consistent throughout. For your font size, make your name 16, all your headings 14, and the rest of your font 12. This will give you a consistent look and have the larger fonts directing the eye to make it easier for the recruiters to go through. Before you start, it may be easier to search for a résumé example for that specific position and use that to build your own.

The things you should have listed are:

- Your name and contact information (bold with font size 14)

  First M. Last (bold with font size 16, everything else font size 12)
  123 Lane, Apt. 1
  City, State Zip
  myemail@gmail.com (use your personal email, not a work email)
  123.456.7890 (use your cell phone number, not a work number)

- Profile summary (bold with font size 14)

  A brief summary of your résumé that is relevant, clear, and concise. Don't use pronouns (the font size 12).

- Professional work experience (bold with font size 14, everything else font size 12)

  Name of company (bold)| *job position or title* (italics)| start and end date (bold)
  Make the name of the company and the dates in bold and the job position or title in italics.
  Start from most recent job and work your way back to establish your work timeline.
  Underneath each company, you will list your achievements in bullet form without pronouns. If you are having trouble, look up "résumé power words and phrases" on Google and try to use them in your achievements as well as key words that you found in the job description. For example:

  Name of company | *job position or title* |
  start and end date

Meticulously rebuilt training regimen and qualification workflow increased qualification times 22 percent.

- Skills/certifications (bold with font size 14, everything else font size 12)

  For certifications: name of school (bold)|*certification obtained* (italics)| the date obtained (bold)
  For skills (if it's software): name of software (bold), *level of experience* (italics). For example: **Microsoft Excel** *(Expert)*
  If you have specific skills but no certifications, remove "certifications" from the subheading. If one of your skills is proficiency in multiple languages, put the language in bold and the level of proficiency in italics using parenthesis as mentioned above.

- Awards (if you have any) (bold with font size 14)

  Use font size 12 with the name of the award in bold and the date obtained in bold.

- Education (bold with font size 14)

  Name of the school (bold) | *city and state (italics)* | start and stop date (bold)
  You should start with the most recent education and end it with your high school diploma and the date.

When you are reading this, it may sound more complicated. Still it is essential that the formatting is consistent throughout your résumé while utilizing the keywords from the job description. The jobs held within five years are the most important, so you must focus more on the relevant achievements and results. Jobs held outside five years are still important but aren't as critical. If you had a gap in your work history, what was the reason for the gap? There are many valid reasons for gaps in your work history, something new mothers typically have to deal with. For some people, there could have been a family emergency or unforeseen circumstance that required you to be elsewhere. Remember, it may not be considered a negative thing. Most companies can be understanding when it comes to those things. Don't mention the gap in your job history unless asked, but be prepared to explain why just in case they do.

If you feel overwhelmed about writing your résumé, feel free to look at templates online and modify them to reflect your work history. If you still don't feel confident, you can go online and find places that will build a professional résumé for you. The website "Indeed" has a résumé creator (LinkedIn also does). Many websites will allow you to make one (although some may charge you to save or print it out, and usually, it's cheap, but prices vary; regardless, it's worth it). Whether you make your own or pay to have one made for you, having a great résumé can be the key to landing a fantastic job with higher pay. If you don't have much experience writing a résumé and you are short on time, paying to have it done may be the better option.

Suppose you decide to pay to have a résumé made for you. In that case, you need to provide the company with all the information we went through earlier and the career page and job descriptions of places you would like to work. This will allow them to utilize the keywords used by those companies and others in the industry to build a targeted résumé. Remember, a great résumé can be the difference between landing your dream job or never hearing back from a company. If you will pay to have a résumé made, read the reviews of the different sites before deciding. You get what you pay for.

PREPARING FOR A JOB INTERVIEW

This section will be much shorter, but it's just as important. Every company has different interview questions they like to ask, but how you answer them is very important. Many of them may be personal, such as asking you to tell them about a time when you had to overcome an obstacle in the workplace. This is just one example, but it throws many people off. The best thing I can recommend is that you go on YouTube and look up "The most common interview questions and how to answer them," and you will get tons of examples that people have been asked about. Most companies will ask questions to see how you would act in a particular situation. In contrast, others may ask job-specific questions to test your knowledge. Please go through them and listen to how they respond, which will significantly help you get through your interview.

Another great tip is to know about the company you are being interviewed by. I've had several interviews where I was asked to tell them what I knew about the company. When I gave a quick synopsis of the company's history, contracts, partnerships, and achievements, it never failed to blow them away. During my interview for my current job, I was offered the position on the spot and told it was the best interview they had done. Not only were they impressed by what I knew about the company, but my answers to their questions were perfect.

They didn't know how nervous I was before the interview because I worried I would mess it up. They didn't know that I spent hours studying the company and practiced going through interview questions with my wife. I wrote down the twenty top interview questions, wrote down my own answer, and studied it religiously. I prepared for my job interview as if I were looking for a final exam. Preparation is everything; if you take your résumé and interview seriously, you won't have any problem landing a good job.

Dress professionally

This may sound self-explanatory, but you would be surprised at how some people show up for a job interview. To keep this very simple, do the following:

- Dress nicely. You can't go wrong with button-up shirt and slacks or a long dress, but even a polo shirt and jeans can be excellent.

- Before your interview, drive by the company and look at how their employees are dressed.
- Look on their website, and you may even find their dress code.

You are a professional and must look the part. You make your first impression as soon as you walk in the door. You should be fine if you dress nicely and have good hygiene. Remember that your posture can give away how you feel (confident, nervous, competent, unsure, etc.), so know the signals you are giving off.

If you have absolutely no fashion sense, search on YouTube for "men's/women's fashion tips for the workplace." Find something that is both professional and looks nice and copy it. How you dress throughout your typical day will reflect on you, and how you dress at work will reflect on the company. Yes, basketball shorts and a T-shirt may be very comfortable. I get it. That is something you want to wear at your home or maybe even at the gym, not in the workplace!

COLLEGE ISN'T THE ONLY ANSWER

Does this sound familiar to you? "You need to go to college to get a good job and be successful in life so you don't end up living on someone's couch." Unfortunately, many parents force the notion onto their children, telling them they need to go to college to succeed. What ends up happening is they feel pressured to go to college, so they attend half-heartedly and find out there isn't any enjoyment in their chosen career path. They switch several times before finishing their degree or dropping out. Others are excited to go to college, do well, and graduate.

The reality for a lot of people coming out of college is now they are carrying a high amount of student loan debt in a field that doesn't make enough to pay it back, on top of having an auto loan they can't afford before realizing they hate the career they ended up with because of the stressful work environment.

In fact, the average time it takes for student loans to be paid off is around twenty years. When you consider all the debt (student loans, auto loans, personal loans, credit cards, mortgages, etc.) they have, most college graduates spend the next thirty to fifty years paying off debt. This problem will only worsen as student loans are backed by the government. Colleges continue to increase the price because they are guaranteed to get paid. Ultimately, the only people it hurts are the ones who believe they can only be successful if they go to college.

Not only can many trade jobs and certifications make more annually than many degrees earn, but you can get most of them in less than six months for only a few thousand dollars, a fraction of the debt you end up with from student loans. If you decide to go to college, don't go for the reason to make more money. By now you should see that making money is much easier than you may have realized, and if you are drowning in debt, you are giving most of it away. To give you a few examples, I will list several trade schools and certifications you can get. The pay varies from location, so I will list the United States average pay. You can search your area and areas you would like to live in. I will use the website "Glassdoor" as it has been rated as one of the best when listing the salaries of different companies. I will use IT-specific certifications, such as "Comptia," to get that information.

DIFFERENT TRADES/CERTIFICATIONS

Trade/ Certifications	Time to complete	Average Hourly Rate/ Range	Total Annual Salary/Range
Plumber	Pre-apprentice program is equal to 2years. Apprentice under a master plumber (if you decide you want to become a master plumber, apply for a journeyman's license).	$22.60–$37.50 based on a forty-hour work week	$47,000–$78,000 (https://www. glassdoor.com/Salaries/ plumber-salary- SRCH_KO0,7.htm)
Master Plumber	4–5 years as a journeyman and then pass the certification test	$36.06–$60.10 based on a forty-hour work week	$75,000–$125,000 (https://www.glassdoor. com/Salaries/master- plumber-salary- SRCH_KO0,14.htm)
Crane Operator	3 weeks of training and then you have to get your NCCCO crane certification	$24.04–$38.94 based on a forty-hour work week	$50,000–$81,000 (https://www.glassdoor. com/Salaries/crane- operator-salary- SRCH_KO0,14.htm)
Electrician	8 months to 2 years, depending on if you go to a trade school or college	$25.49–$42.79 based on a forty-hour work week	$53,000–$89,000 (https://www. glassdoor.com/Salaries/ electrician-salary- SRCH_KO0,11.htm)
Wind Turbine Technician	7 months	$25.96–$38.94 based on a forty-hour work week	$54,000–$81,000 (https://www.glassdoor. com/Salaries/wind- turbine-technician-salary- SRCH_KO0,23.htm)

Commercial Driver	3 weeks	$28.37–$45.19 based on a forty-hour work week	$59,000–$94,000 (https://www.glassdoor.com/Salaries/truck-driver-salary-SRCH_KO0,12.htm)
Heavy Equipment Mechanic	1–2 years	$28.37–$41.83 based on a forty-hour work week	$59,000–$87,000 (https://www.glassdoor.com/Salaries/heavy-equipment-mechanic-salary-SRCH_KO0,24.htm0
HVAC Technician	1.5 years trade school, 2-5 years through college	$23.08–$36.06 based on a forty-hour work week	$48,000–$75,000 (https://www.glassdoor.com/Salaries/hvac-technician-salary-SRCH_KO0,15.htm)
Auto Body Technician	51–54 weeks	$21.63–$33.65 based on a forty-hour work week	$45,000–$70,000 (https://www.glassdoor.com/Salaries/auto-body-technician-salary-SRCH_KO0,20.htm)
Welder	6–18 months through a technical school, 2 years at a college	$22.60–$33.17 based on a forty-hour work week	$47,000–$69,000 (https://www.glassdoor.com/Salaries/welder-salary-SRCH_KO0,6.htm)
Carpenter	You can start entry level, but you need four years of experience to become a licensed carpenter.	$20.19–$31.73 based on a forty-hour work week	$42,000–$66,000 (https://www.glassdoor.com/Salaries/carpenter-salary-SRCH_KO0,9.htm)
Automotive Technician	10 months	$21.63–$33.17 based on a forty-hour work week	$45,000–$69,000 (https://www.glassdoor.com/Salaries/automotive-technician-salary-SRCH_KO0,21.htm)

Auto Mechanic	2–5 years for an automotive technician to earn an ASE certification	$24.52–$36.06 based on a forty-hour work week	$51,000–$75,000 (https://www.glassdoor.com/Salaries/auto-mechanic-salary-SRCH_KO0,13.htm)
Fiber Optics	2–4 weeks for many of the certifications; 1–3 months on-the-job training if you started at an entry-level position	$22.12–$35.10 based on a forty-hour work week	$46,000–$73,000 (https://www.glassdoor.com/Salaries/fiber-optic-technician-salary-SRCH_KO0,22.htm)
Comptia A+	Anywhere from 1–4 weeks as an average	$21.63–$34.13 based on a forty-hour work week	$45,000–$71,000 (https://www.glassdoor.com/Salaries/a-certified-computer-technician-salary-SRCH_KO0,31.htm)
CompTIA Network+	2 weeks through a boot camp or 2–4 weeks self-study and passing the certification	$36.06 based on a forty-hour work week	Wide range, but with an average of $75k (https://www.payscale.com/research/US/Certification=CompTIA_Network%2B/Salary)
CompTIA Security+	2 weeks through a boot camp or 2–4 weeks self-study and passing the certification	$39.90 based on a forty-hour work week	Wide range, but with an average of $83k (https://www.payscale.com/research/US/Certification=CompTIA_Security%2B/Salary)

Some people will see this and be upset because they still live with the notion that you should go to college, but that information isn't as useful as it used to be, so I will say this. Don't go to college if your only goal is to earn more money or become successful. Go to college if that career field is something that you really want to work in, knowing that it might not pay enough for what you need. I have a strong appreciation for teachers, but unfortunately, their pay is horrible, and depending on the age group and location they teach, it can become very stressful. Many teachers must rely on a second or summer job because they don't make enough to cover their expenses. Maybe teaching was their passion and they would do it for free if they had to, and that's okay. Unfortunately, many college graduates end up becoming depressed and stuck in a job they hate with debt that takes thirty to fifty years to pay off.

Please don't allow your family to pressure you into college, and parents are the worst when it comes to this. That mindset came from when student debt was significantly less and you could live on a single income while retiring at forty. It's 2023 when I wrote this, and things have drastically changed since your parents went to school. Truly consider why you want to go and if it's right for you. If you decide to go, start at a community college for most core classes as it's much cheaper. Use apps, like Scholly, which allow you to fill in your personal information and tell you every scholarship you meet the requirements for. Apply for all of them. Also please apply for the ones you don't meet the criteria; chances are you will get approved for some of them.

Once your debt is paid off, it's time to start saving and investing. You already have an emergency fund, so now you want to start saving for things like a house, a vehicle, vacations, or whatever else you can think of. It would be best if you also started investing, which is covered in a later chapter. As you did with your emergency fund, save for those items separately so it has already been budgeted and accounted for. Saving for a down payment on a house is a perfect choice. Saving funds for a vehicle (consider buying one around 5 years old) and/or vehicle repairs is another excellent choice. Saving for a vacation allows you to accumulate funds, so you already have the funds accounted for when you decide to go on vacation. This is when you start planning for your future!

Summary

So far, you learned how to make a personal financial statement and used that information to reduce expenses and increase income. Then you learned to pay off your debt using either the avalanche or the snowball method. Once debt-free, you will have cash flow to purchase assets to generate income. You will now also be able to benefit from using a credit card properly so you can improve your credit score and start earning free rewards and money. This is where all the hard work is done, and you get to start building a future. Please leave a review and let me know how this information has changed your life! There is a lot more left, so keep reading and enjoy the new life you have started for yourself!

Instead of going to college, you can specialize in a trade or certification to develop a strong skill set and save your income to go toward a down payment on a home with multiple rooms. You then can utilize house hacking to not only have your mortgage paid off but also have positive cash flow while the people who are going to college are increasing the amount of student loan debt they have. Once you have your mortgage paid halfway down, refinance to reduce the monthly payments to increase your cash flow and purchase another property and do the same thing. By the time someone would have finished a four-year degree with lots of debt, you would already be working on purchasing a second property while generating positive cash flow from your first one while working in a specialized trade with zero debt. Instead of your income going toward debt payments, they are going into assets that are appreciating in value and generate positive cash flow. Work smarter, not harder.

CHAPTER 6

CREDIT SCORE, CREDIT CARDS, AND REWARDS

I initially didn't intend to write anything about this topic for the book. I planned on writing an entire book dedicated to credit cards, credit scores, and the rewards by thoroughly reviewing each one and selecting the top thirty to share with people so they can have the best information possible to compare to. I ultimately decided to add this information because of how many people this can help and because having a great credit score can save you hundreds of thousands throughout your life because you can get lower-interest rates.

The purpose of this book is to help as many people as possible. I want this book to be something that can change the lives of the people who read it and take action. I want to help people achieve their dreams and live without stress and struggle. Misuse of credit cards can ruin lives, friendships, families, and relationships. Now that you are debt-free or on the path to becoming debt-free, I want you to start benefiting from your current lifestyle in ways you may not have known existed.

There are three main credit bureaus that you need to be familiar with: Experian, Equifax, and Transunion. Whenever you applied for a loan, credit card, mortgage, apartment, or rental application, you probably had a credit check run. Those three bureaus I mentioned store your credit information and history to let companies see your credit history in the form of a FICO score. The purpose of the credit score is to determine the amount of risk you represent. Depending on your score, you will pay different interest rates. Lower scores mean you will pay the highest rates while higher scores tell you will pay the lowest interest rates. Your credit score is one of the determining factors on whether or not you get approved for a loan.

A score less than 579 is considered very poor. A score between 580–669 is considered to be fair. A score between 670–739 is considered good. A score between 740–799 is considered very good, and a score from 800–850 is considered exceptional. In a little bit, I will tell you how these numbers are accumulated. Still it is essential to know the ranges because it can let you know where you fall. If you need a loan for any reason, it may be better to wait until you are in a higher range to get a lower-interest rate.

Your FICO score

- Payment history makes up 35 percent of your score and has the biggest impact on your score.
- Credit utilization makes up 30 percent of your score.
- Age of accounts makes up 15 percent of your score.
- Type of debt makes up 10 percent of your score.
- Number of credit inquiries makes up 10 percent of your score.

Payment history (35 percent) will be the history of your payments (did you pay them on time or were you late and how often). Certain things have a more significant impact on your score. This information stays on the system for seven years, so making all your payments on time is crucial. Missed payments can severely reduce your credit score. When you are reducing your expenses and increasing your income, the first thing you want to do is make sure you *never* miss a payment. Set up automatic payments on as many things as possible and write down the dates they will pull from your account. When paying off your debts, always ensure you are within your budget and do whatever it takes to pay on time. The extra cash flow can be a godsend.

Credit utilization (30 percent) is the total amount (as a percentage) of the credit you are using. What is essential about credit utilization is knowing how much of your total credit limit you can use without negatively affecting your account. If your total available credit limit was $15,000, you want to ensure you never use more than 30 percent of it (which would be $4,500 for this example). If your total was from three separate credit cards (credit card A has a $10,000 limit, credit card B has a $3,000 limit, credit card C has a $2,000 limit for a total of $15,000), some people recommend not using more than 10 percent of any card or 30 percent of your total. This information is a myth; the only number that matters is your credit utilization being less than 30 percent of your total. Spreading it out between different cards doesn't help your credit score, but using multiple cards can add to that stress if you are already struggling to manage all the payments you have to make. The only advantage to using various credit cards would be to take advantage of the benefits provided by that card (more on this later). If you close your credit card account, you will also reduce the total credit available. It is recommended to keep your accounts open, which I tend to agree with as closing them can potentially lower your credit score.

Age of accounts (15 percent) is essential, and one of the reasons I plan on adding my children as authorized users when they get older is to get them their own cards down the road. This will allow them to benefit from my credit history as it will boost their credit score. It is a good way for them to build a credit score without acquiring debt. When it comes to you, keep your accounts open even if you don't use the card anymore. The longer your account has been available, the better it is for your credit score and history. Opening too many accounts at once can lower your score, so it is better to space them out. I have six credit cards, but I only use one (it is a fantastic card with incredible benefits). I will continue leaving the accounts open. Occasionally, I will use one of them and immediately pay the balance off. Hence, the card still shows as being actively used, so later on, I can ask for a credit increase to raise my total credit available.

The type of debt (10 percent) affects your credit based on your debt. A credit card is considered revolving credit, which typically has high-interest rates. Service credit is a type of debt like your phone and internet services. Installment debts are things like mortgages and student loans. The final kind of debt is called open debt, which could be charge cards that require you to pay the entire balance at the end of the month. Missing a payment on any debt will reduce your credit score, but having different kinds of debt is one of the things that can actually help it. A good combination is a mortgage, phone and internet services, and credit cards. If you want to see how you are doing in this area, you can go to Experian.com or download the app, and you can access all your information and tips to improve them. Each category will have its own score, and I find the app useful. The other bureaus have apps as well, but Experian has been the one I prefer.

Number of credit inquiries (10 percent) is a score based on how many credit checks you received. There are challenging and soft inquiries; it is essential to know the difference since hard inquiries drop your credit score and soft inquiries do not. The Experian app, for example, allows me to check my actual credit score whenever I want. When you check your own credit score, it is treated as a soft inquiry. If you have ever received a "preapproved loan" offer in the mail, that is the result of a soft inquiry. A hard inquiry would be when you are filling out loan applications, and they run your credit information. Mortgages, auto loans, and credit cards count as a hard inquiry. If you are buying a home and shopping for the best rates, you have to be sure you are doing your "shopping" within thirty days from when they run your credit. During the thirty days, you can call multiple lenders to find the best price, which will only count as a single hit instead of numerous. When I first decided to buy a home, I made the mistake of shopping for the "best rates" for two months. My credit took a decent drop after that (which eventually went back up).

One of the things you can do to immediately boost your credit score is to pull up your credit reports and go through them. If there is anything negative on your credit reports, you should dispute it. If the credit bureau cannot verify that the damaging information is accurate within a reasonable amount of time (I believe that period is thirty days), they must remove it from your record. The only time you shouldn't do it is if the information is around six years old because if it is verified to be accurate, it resets the time back to day one (things stay on your record for seven years).

CREDIT SCORE SUMMARY

This is a quick summary to make it simple:

- Make all your payments on time (35 percent of your score is based off this).
- Don't use more than 30 percent of your total available credit (30 percent of your score is based off this).
- Keep your accounts open even if rarely used (15 percent of your score is based off this).
- Multiple types of debt are actually a good thing (10 percent of your score is based off this). (Don't accumulate debt just to try to have multiple types of debt. This is the least important part of the credit score and just having two different types is sufficient).
- Don't apply for a lot of credit cards and loans. If you are shopping, condense the amount of time spend doing so (10 percent of your score is based off this).
- Dispute all negative information on your credit reports. You may end up getting the item removed from it if the bureau doesn't verify it within a certain amount of time!

CREDIT CARD USAGE AND REWARDS

Once you are out of debt, there isn't a reason to continue using a debit card unless it's for ATM usage or making payments on things that don't allow you to pay with a credit card. The benefits of a sound credit card are excellent, and a debit card doesn't provide you any benefits. Credit cards are also more secure, and the customer service is usually outstanding because they want to keep you as a loyal customer!

The important things to remember when using a credit card are as follows:

- Treat it like a debit card and only use it if you can pay it off immediately.
- Pay the balance in full as soon as it posts or before the end of the billing cycle (no interest will be charged if you pay before the end of the billing cycle. Please note that the end of the billing cycle is different from the end of the month).
- Please don't use more than 30 percent of your available credit limit (we discussed this earlier).
- Get a card with rewards that you would utilize.
- Minimum payments only cover the interest and don't pay off the balance.

It sounds easy, and it really is that simple. The biggest problem most people make is they only make minimum payments on their card, which only goes toward interest. Then they continue using the card, and the balance goes up. You must make minimum payments to pay it off. I recommend doing what I stated earlier and paying off the balance in full when it posts to your account or before the end of the billing cycle.

The *only* time you should make a minimum payment is if you are doing so strategically (if you are paying off your debt using the snowball or avalanche method, you will pay the minimum payment on everything *except* the one with the lowest amount [Snowball] or the one with the highest interest rates [avalanche]). Also there are short-term investment strategies where you can use a credit card to purchase a particular investment and then sell that specific investment for profit. You then use those profits earned to pay off the card and keep the rest, essentially using the bank's money to make money for you and earning you free rewards from using your credit card. I don't recommend you use this method unless you know what you are doing.

I know someone who builds custom computers for his clients by taking their specifications, figuring out the cost to purchase and have it delivered, and then giving them the total price, including labor. If they agree, they pay him, and he orders everything with his credit card and then pays off the balance as soon as it posts. His side hustle alone has earned him several thousand in rewards from credit card usage over three years, not to mention all the other transactions he makes with his credit card that also earn him points.

Most credit cards with great benefits have an annual fee, and some don't have a payment at all, but the rewards are less. That is beyond the scope of the book. Still I plan to write a book that goes over every excellent credit card and all the benefits provided by each, along with a list that I would consider the best. With so many choices, you need to consider the fees associated with the card versus the benefits they provide.

The card my wife and I use is the American Express Gold card. While the annual fee may scare off some people ($245 annually), I find the card to be perfect for what I do (the American Express Platinum is also a great card, but it has a higher annual fee than the gold, and the additional benefits aren't as relevant for what I need). Your purchases earn you points based on how much you spend, what you spend it on, and where you purchase from. Those points can be traded for cash, gift cards, flight miles, etc. American Express Gold allows you to get discounted airline tickets, hotels, and many others if you purchase through their app or website. Within one year, I earned enough points to buy two round-trip tickets to the other side of the world that would be entirely free for me! Some people use it to pay for their vacation trips or airline tickets. Others use it to buy their families gifts or save it for emergencies.

I get all those benefits I mentioned. American Express also gives me $10 a month toward certain restaurants ($120 a year) and $10 a month toward Uber/Uber Eats ($120 a year). Since I fly regularly for business, I get discounted tickets (or free if I want to use my points) and a free Uber ride from the airport. If I wanted to use my points to get cash back, I could pay off several annual fees just from one year of using it. When you use credit cards to benefit you, shop around first. Find the one that gives you the rewards you will benefit the most from. The American Express credit cards are unique, and I recommend them to anyone.

There may be better ones for you than this card. Still with the large number available, I recommend you search YouTube for "credit cards with the best benefits" and see what you get. There are thousands of videos because people worldwide realize how fantastic credit cards can be when used correctly. As I mentioned, I plan on writing a book that covers all these, but I want you to check out YouTube first. Not only is it free, but you can also get the information in a shorter amount of time. While I wouldn't mind making extra by selling a book, I aim to help you have all the information to change your life.

CHAPTER 7

INVESTING IN STOCKS

By now, you realize that your life is heading differently. You are no longer struggling to get by but the person who always finds a way to achieve their goals. But what are your goals? What does success mean to you? Many people never give much thought to their future because they are struggling so much in the present moment. Now that you are debt-free, utilizing credit cards improves your credit, gives you amazing rewards, and earns you money. Now you have your entire life ahead of you. What are your plans for retirement?

This is one of the significant problems facing Americans because most people need more money invested or saved for retirement. This is one of the problems I am trying to solve. It doesn't matter how old you are; it's never too late to start investing. Everyone dies, and most of us don't know how long we have. If I die within the next five years, how does it affect my family? I don't know how long I have, but I do know that I want to become the best version of myself and teach my kids the things I wish I knew as a teenager. Regardless of how much money I can leave them with, if I can leave them with the knowledge and fundamentals to become successful on their own, then I will have succeeded. By writing this book, I'm effectively giving my children and future grandchildren all the tools necessary to become successful. Not only do I want this for my family, but I want this for everyone. I want everyone to become successful and to grow.

I hope you purchased this book while you are still young because it will allow you to use compounding interest for longer. The younger you are, the more time will work on your side. If you are older, don't worry too much; you still have time to build something unique. Compound interest benefits everyone who utilizes it, making it essential to understand. It is essentially your money-earning money for you. Compound interest is more easily explained through an example.

Suppose you invested $10,000 in an account with 10 percent annual interest. If you never invested money into that account again, it would continue growing. In one year, 10 percent interest would increase your account by $1,000 for $11,000. The following year, a 10 percent interest would now grow your account by $1,100 for $12,100. Year three would increase to $13,310, and if you let that $10,000 that you started with grow over twenty years, that $10,000 grows into $67,275.

Now, you might look at that and think those numbers are small, but if you notice, they grow larger yearly. Now let's imagine that your account had $100,000 and you decided to stop investing in it and let it grow. What would it look like in twenty years with the market average of 10.5 percent? Let me show you.

Time in Years	Interest Gained	End Balance
1	$10,500	$110,500
2	$11,602.50	$122,102.5
3	$12,820.76	$134,923.26
4	$14,166.94	$149,090.21
5	$15,654.47	$164,744.68
6	$17,298.19	$182,042.87
7	$19,114.50	$201,157.37
8	$21,121.52	$222,278.89
9	$23,339.28	$245,618.18
10	$25,789.91	$271,408.08
11	$28,497.12	$299,905.93

12	$31,490.12	$331,396.06
13	$34,796.59	$366,192.64
14	$38,450.23	$404,642.87
15	$42,487.50	$447,130.37
16	$46,948.69	$494,079.06
17	$51,878.30	$545,957.36
18	$57,325.52	$603,282.88
19	$63,344.70	$666,627.59
20	$69,995.90	$736,623.48

Looking at these two examples, you only made the initial investment and let compound interest and time do the work. If you continue to invest every month, you can accelerate the growth in your account in less time. You may have a goal of becoming a millionaire. Before you read this book, you might have been like I was before I changed my life. I thought being a millionaire was something impossible for me. But guess what? Becoming a millionaire isn't that hard. In fact, if people had the proper knowledge at a young age, most of the people you know could also be millionaires. Let me give you an example.

The US stock market grows at an average rate of 10.5 percent a year (the reason I used 10.5 percent in my previous example). If you decided to invest $1,000 each month for the next twenty-three years with an initial balance of zero, you would have $1,021,573.07 in your brokerage account. Suppose you go back to the chapter talking about increasing your income. In that case, you will understand what I said about making money is easier than most people realize. You can accomplish whatever you set out to do. You have to have goals and a plan to reach them. You can download a compound interest calculator on your phone through the App Store, which can help you visualize just how powerful compounding interest is. The earlier you start investing, the better.

There are many different ways to invest, and each investment has many strategies you can use. Most self-made millionaires earned their millions through real estate and investing in the stock market. Many other types of investments exist, but these two are always at the top of the list. I recommend that you consider using both. If your company has a 401(k), I suggest utilizing its tax benefits. The 401(k)s are Roth eligible, meaning you can pay tax at the time of investment and let your account grow. Because you paid the taxes up-front, you won't have to pay taxes on the growth! I recommend maxing this out, investing in a Roth IRA and maxing this out. The tax benefits alone can save you hundreds of thousands of dollars. If your company doesn't offer a 401(k), you can find several 401(k) options to work with online.

Each company has different options as to the stock available to choose from. While some have many options, others have very few. They all have many portfolios to choose from if you want to go that route. If you don't feel like investing or have no interest in learning about the stock market, talk with the company and figure out which option you want to go with. If your company offers to match a certain percentage, even better (my company offers a 5 percent match, and the one I worked for prior had a 4 percent match). I know many people who don't feel comfortable about investing because of the overwhelming amount of information. It makes it very hard to know where to begin.

Before talking about investing, I want to review a few things that will make the process easier by automating your investments and taking the emotional side of funding out of the equation. Removing the emotions from investing allows you to be more disciplined with your investing decisions.

DOLLAR-COST AVERAGING

The first thing I want to talk about is dollar-cost averaging. Many people try to time the market to buy low and sell high, but most people believe high and sell low. Dollar-cost averaging allows you to take the emotions out of it by investing the same amount each month into stocks. It doesn't matter if the price is high or low because you will support it regardless. When the price drops, you can purchase more shares of that stock with the same amount. If the price increases, you can buy fewer shares of that stock with the same amount of money.

This will grow your money faster over time because when you buy the stocks for a lower price, you acquire more shares. With the general market trending up more than 70 percent of the time, the stock value increases over time, and you earn more money because you will have more shares. With the stock prices rising and falling, this method reduces your risk and accelerates growth over time. Not only is it one of the best methods for investing, but you can also set it up automatically so you don't have to worry about it. Benjamin Graham, Warren Buffet, and many other investors who were considered among the greatest investors in the world utilized this method. The best way to diversify your portfolio is to invest in low-cost index funds and/or ETFs using dollar-cost averaging. Some ETFs track index funds, so check all your options before deciding which one you choose. Each platform is different, and some ETFs aren't available on other platforms.

DOLLAR-COST AVERAGING ACCELERANT

A way to make dollar-cost averaging even better is to allocate a certain amount of income each month for use when the market drops by a significant amount (set it aside and keep growing this amount until you find an excellent opportunity to use it). This number entirely depends on you. When the price drops by whatever percentage you decide to go with (a 10 percent drop as an example), *you could use these saved funds to purchase more of it, so when the price returns back to normal, you already made a 10 percent increase on your investment* (you can do this with specific companies in your portfolio, which can make a massive difference long-term).

I have a list of solid companies I monitor each quarter that are separate from my actual portfolio. I continuously monitor my portfolio to see if one of my companies needs to be replaced. I would only return a company in my portfolio if its fundamentals have changed, its financial health throws red flags, or management changes and the company loses value.

Many panic when the prices drop and start selling their stocks, but this is the best time for you to invest. As long as the companies continue to be high-value, dips in the stock prices are essentially discounts that will accelerate the growth of your account. Let's say you wanted to buy the latest iPhone but delayed it because the price was too high. A month later, you see that the price dropped 12 percent, which allows you to get what you want for a lower price. A few days after buying your iPhone, the sale ends, and it is back at its original price. Think of a price drop as getting your favorite stock at a discount! This is what makes dollar-cost averaging and the abovementioned technique so powerful. It makes the volatility of the market work for you. Day traders always try to time the market to buy low and sell high, but over 90 percent fail long-term. If you use these two methods together, your account will grow exponentially.

By the way, I don't recommend day trading, especially if you are new to investing. As I said, most day traders fail over the long term. The best thing you can do is invest in either ETFs or index funds every month because of the diversification they bring and the low cost in fees. When you are more knowledgeable at researching companies and selecting high-quality companies, switching from ETFs to individual companies can be a great move that can lead to higher returns (with more risks), or you can use a combination to get high returns with minimal risks!

With that being said, there are other ways you can immediately start investing today that are automated and don't require additional work after setting it up. An app called *Acorns* is a micro-investing app that allows you to invest your "change" into an ETF (exchange-traded funds) that you select when you set up your account. An ETF is a diversified collection of assets from companies traded like stocks. Investing in an ETF allows you to invest in hundreds of companies simultaneously. Because of the diversity, it has less risk and lower fees because it isn't actively managed like you would get from a mutual fund. They are perfect for someone who doesn't want to become more involved in learning how to invest in the stock market investing but wants to get the benefits and the gains in a safer/lower-risk way. Because of their diversity, most ETFs end up outperforming individual stocks.

When I said invest your change, they round up your purchase to the following dollar amount and invest the difference. If I went into 7-Eleven and purchased a drink for $2.87, Acorns would round up to the nearest dollar and invest the difference of $0.13 in this example. If your total purchase price was $1.99, Acorns would invest $0.01 cents from your account. If your purchase price was $4, they would invest $1 from your account. Acorns has recently added many more options to their platform so you can now invest "double" the change, automatically invest every month into your portfolio, invest one-time amounts, and many other options. It is a decent platform for automated investing that makes it perfect for people who are brand-new or don't have the funds to invest. Even when you start gaining experience in supporting and using other platforms, their unique method of financing your "change" is an excellent reason to consider using them even if you invest in different platforms. Later on, I will give my opinion and recommendations as my opinion may surprise you.

ASSET ALLOCATION

Asset allocation is one of the most important things when it comes to investing. It doesn't matter how much your account grows if you lose it all. You have to have a good balance of risk and securities. A rule of thumb has been around for a while where you use your age as the percentage to be invested in bonds (your securities/bond section). If you are thirty, you would want your portfolio to be 70 percent invested in risk/growth stocks and 30 percent invested in securities/bonds. I believe this to be decent advice; however, stocks have more than doubled the returns of bonds over the last eighty years. Bonds are considered safe because if you get Treasury Inflation-Protection Securities (TIPS), the interest rises to match inflation. You won't lose your money, but you won't gain much. I want to clarify that placing a portion in bonds is good advice even though I don't do the same. I will discuss the reason why later on.

If investing in ETFs or index funds, you can put more emphasis on the risk portion of your portfolio because it is already diversified by hundreds of companies. For example, Warren Buffet recommended putting 10 percent in short-term government bonds and 90 percent into an S&P index fund. Even though his ratio seems more aggressive (90%/10% compared to 70%/30%), diversification within an ETF or index fund minimizes your risk.

As you saw in an earlier chapter, making money is easy. Keeping it is much more complicated. Whatever ratio you want to use is entirely up to you, but base it on how much risk you are willing to accept. This method will give you steady gains over time by keeping your portfolio simple and diverse. This is the key to long-term success, and you can automate it, so it is entirely passive! Suppose your portfolio's risk/growth portion takes off and your percentages are incorrect, in that case, you can rebalance your portfolio to bring it back where you want.

DIFFERENCES BETWEEN ETFs, INDEX FUNDS, AND MUTUAL FUNDS

Before going into more detail, I wanted to discuss ETFs (exchange-traded funds), index funds, and mutual funds. They have a lot of similarities because investing in them allows you to own many different stocks (think of it as a bundle; you purchase one stock that is made up of hundreds of different stocks). This gives you diversification, which is great for new investors. As Warren Buffet stated, "Diversification is protection against ignorance." Before you take that in a negative light, it's true. There are thousands of companies, and being able to identify the best ones that are undervalued or have amazing potential isn't as easy as people think. If you are unable to identify these, diversification through ETFs, index funds, or mutual funds will still allow you to invest and grow your money. This will allow you to benefit from the growth of the market as you continue to learn about how to identify individual companies based on whatever strategy you believe is right for you.

When it comes to the difference between these, mutual funds are actively managed and have higher fees (even their performance isn't usually better as most underperform the market). Index funds and ETFs typically have lower fees and a better performance because of that. Out of the three groups, index funds and ETFs tend to have the lowest expenses which make them better options. They have lower fees because they are passively managed, meaning they are typically rebalanced (actively managed funds are constantly buying and selling stocks, trying to outperform the market; however, they are taxable events each time, and you are also paying a higher fee, which results in underperformance). With index funds, you can only buy them once a day when the trading day ends. Along with that, they can only be sold after the trading day ends.

ETFs are different because they trade like stocks and are more liquid as a result. They have lower fees than mutual funds and have similar or slightly higher fees than index funds. Some index funds have minimum requirements when it comes to deposits while ETFs allow you to buy as many as you want with as much or as little capital you decide to invest. Some brokerages charge a commission for making trades, but some do not. Personally, I like ETFs out of the three options the best because of the wide variety of ETFs available.

How to find great companies to invest in

Throughout this portion of the book, you may have noticed that I stressed the importance of investing in solid, high-quality companies. Still I didn't tell you how to do it. That is what this section is going to help you with. There are many ways and methods, so I will talk about the ones I use and why. I use various techniques to determine which companies I invest in, starting with the simplest and working my way down.

VISUAL OBSERVATION AND PERSONAL EXPERIENCE

This is a powerful method that is easy to use and understand, and I learned about it while researching Peter Lynch. He discusses this method in many interviews and in several of his books. Essentially, you can easily identify great companies by just paying attention to what's around you. If you go into a store, you can easily see what stores are full of people with in-demand products and which ones are empty. You can identify them by the things people wear and the things they use.

As an example, I went to the mall with my wife yesterday, and we walked around for several hours. There were many stores selling electronics, such as an Apple store, Samsung, Acer, and one that sold computers of all brands. Of all the stores, Apple was the one that was completely packed the entire time we were at the mall. Not only was it packed, but almost everyone there had several Apple products. I prefer Samsung over Apple in regard to phones, but Apple does an exceptional job at integrating their products to work efficiently together, and most people who own an Apple product actually own several. Not only do they have high quality phones, but they also have computers, earphones, smart watches, Apple TV, and many other products and services. They use higher quality parts (part of the reason they cost more) and great customer service. There branding is impeccable and has become a status symbol. Even though there isn't much difference between the iPhone 12 and 15, the demand is so high just because people want to own the newest model.

When you find a company that stands out like this, write it down so you can look it up later. Later on, you want to compare it to its competitors to see who does it better. To show how easy this process can be, talk to children. I asked my nine-year-old what is his favorite thing to do, and he said playing the Nintendo Switch. All his friends play the Switch, and many of the games are geared toward children, and it's enjoyed by many adults as well. Nintendo owns the rights to many games, has a long history of producing high quality games, and dominant the handheld gaming market. I asked my son if he knew other companies who are also made games, and he instantly mentioned the PlayStation (owned by Sony) and Xbox (owned by Microsoft). When I was in the military, the Nintendo Switch was the most popular because of the mobility that you get with a handheld system. Even when traveling around the world, you see the Nintendo Switch selling in the majority of stores, and there are always people looking through the games. While Microsoft and Sony are competitors in regard to gaming consoles, the Nintendo Switch is the number one company for handheld systems. Once you identify a good company, add it to your list.

Using the example my son gave with Nintendo, I would then look at the company's performance and financial statements. At the time of writing this, Nintendo is up 10.01 percent year to date (YTD), up 32.44 percent for its one-year returns, and 101.72 percent over the past five years. Now that I see the company has been performing well, I then look through their balance sheets and income statements (covered in the next two sections). Using the current ratio, I see that they have a current ratio of 4.08. Banks typically prefer companies to fall between 1.2 and 2 as below that means they could potentially be over-leveraged (utilizing more debt to grow their business than what would be considered safe) or they have a lot more debt due within a year than they have the funds available to pay it off. I will discuss this more in a later section, but it is used to determine the company's ability to pay their short-term debts. Greater than a ratio of two indicates that the company may not be utilizing their available capital as efficiently as they could, meaning they could be using it to grow their company or invest it into research and development for newer products.

One thing to point out is that when you use Yahoo Finance and click on "Financials," you can look at their earnings compared to their earnings on an annual or quarterly basis. At the time of me writing this, I can see that from 2021 to 2023, both their earnings and revenue have been slowly decreasing each year. While normally I prefer a stock to show growth in revenue and earnings year over year, some companies go through periods of time where they under-perform. When you go on Google and look up the future plans for Nintendo, I immediately saw that Nintendo hasn't released any official information in regard to the release of a new console; however, the Nintendo Switch was released seven years ago. Nintendo typically releases a new console every five to six years, meaning we are due for a new release soon. The handheld market for gaming systems will always exist, and their most direct competitor is the Steam Deck, which is owned by Valve and not publicly traded as it's a private company.

I believe the announcement of a new console will generate a lot of growth and demand for Nintendo, and I expect that announcement to come any time from now until a few years. Even though the price is currently trading at its fifty-two-week high and many people think it's currently overvalued, I disagree. This company, in my opinion, is actually undervalued and a great company to hold long-term. The release of the next console will dramatically improve the demand for their products. This company will be around for a long time, and they have a history of releasing consoles and games that are high quality and high in demand.

In conclusion, pay attention to what's around you, invest in what you know, and try to understand the patents/products/services a company has and make sure you understand why they are performing the way they are and why they are either growing or declining. The reason their revenue and earnings have slowly declined for the last few years is due to the console having been out for the last seven years, and the majority of their fan base already owns the console, meaning the majority of their income is coming from their game sales at the moment. Nintendo is slower to release newer consoles, so they tend to reflect that in their stock chart prior to a new release. A new release will increase their earnings in console sales, plus the income from the profit the games produce. This isn't always the case as the Wii U wasn't very successful, but that is why we looked at their balance sheet (to see how a company's financial health looks to reduce the risk in case the company experiences hardship). Even if their next console isn't successful, I'm confident that this company will be around for a long time. Without knowing anything about stocks or investing, my son understood that the Nintendo Switch is popular and has many games that are easy to learn and play. He also said people play it in his school and it's easy to bring with him. When I was a kid, this was the reason the Game Boy Advance was my favorite console.

If my son were to invest in companies he already knows something about and he knows how to identify their competitors, he would actually be successful. Another product he mentioned was the iPhone because everyone he knows or sees on TV is using one (including my wife and I). He would be ahead of many investors, who tend to buy based off their current price alone, hoping to buy low and sell high. By instead investing into high-quality companies long-term, you greatly reduce your risk.

BALANCE SHEETS AND INCOME STATEMENTS

The next step will take a little time, but it's an important step that shouldn't be skipped. You will take your list of companies that you like. You will go through their most recent balance sheets and income statements (you can quickly find this information on Yahoo Finance by typing in the company name and selecting "Financials"). The companies make the information public, so finding this information is relatively easy. The first time you look at these can be confusing or overwhelming, so I will explain each significant portion very simply. I recommend you read through it thoroughly and reread it while going through an actual balance sheet and income statement. Not only will it make a lot more sense, but it will also help you retain the information.

YAHOO FINANCE AND NINTENDO

Before I explain what you will see on those documents, I want to let you know that you can see all this on Yahoo Finance. If you download the mobile app, it will open up to a screen that is showing a spot where you can customize alerts, set a watch list for stocks you have interest in, news about companies, and a search bar. If you type in the name of the company in the search bar, it will show the company and the ticker symbol (sometimes there are very similar ones, so pay attention to which one you click on). Because we just used Nintendo in the example above, type "Nintendo" in the search bar once you download the Yahoo Finance app. The first thing you will see is the stock's current price and a chart. YTD is year to date, as stated before, and it shows you the price change throughout the current year. One year will show the price movement over the last 365 days. The five years shows the price movement over the past five years. This is a quick way to check out the performance visually. Maximum shows the company's price movement throughout their history. If you select "Max" on Nintendo, you will see that 1995 to 1999 was relatively flat, 1999 to mid-2002 you had some growth that returned back to the same price it was from 1995 to 1999. It wasn't until the end of 2005 where the price began to pick up until 2008 where the price began to drop once again. In 2010, the price was similar to where it was in 1995–1999 but began to increase around 2015. Ever since 2015, the company has shown great growth that is much different than its earlier history.

Before I talk about what happened during these time periods, I want to talk more about Yahoo Finance to make it easier for you to use and understand. When you scroll down from the chart, you will see the categories of Summary, Analysis, and Financials. Each of these have the option to "View More." Clicking "View More" on the Summary tab gives you everything you need to know all in one page. If you wanted to look more in depth at their balance sheet, income statement, or cash flow statement, you click on Financials and click on "View More." Under the Analysis tab, it gives recommendations based on different analysts' opinions on whether they recommend buying, holding, or selling. If you Click on "View More," you can see earnings and revenue estimates for the current year and the projection for the future. They usually provide a low and high estimate, but the wider the gap, the less predictable because no one really knows what to expect. With Nintendo, the low and high estimate for earnings and revenue show a projected gain, and the low and highs are exactly the same (low and high for earnings are the same, and low and high for revenue is the same). This shows that the analyst feel pretty confident about the projected price; however, for Nintendo, it shows that there is only one analyst. I myself don't use the Analysis tab but wanted to make you aware what to find there.

Now getting back to Nintendo, let's take a look at what happened during the times it went up in value as well as when it dropped to have a better understanding of why the price moves the way it does. The Game Boy Color came out in 1998 and was very popular. When I was in school, everyone seemed to have one, and everyone was playing Pokémon. I didn't have one at the time, but you couldn't go anywhere without seeing someone's child with one in their hands. Although the Game Boy Color was successful, many other companies were releasing consoles around the same time, and when the Nintendo GameCube was released, it was competing against the PlayStation 2 and the Xbox. The Nintendo Wii was released in 2006 and was a great success that brought it to the highest stock price it had seen (in 2020, it finally beat that high but barely). The hype of the Nintendo Wii slowly died down as its graphics weren't as good as that of its previous console (GameCube) and because of the release of consoles from their competitors.

With the release of the Wii U, however, there wasn't as much success. The competition continued to put out more in-demand products, such as the PlayStation 4 and the Xbox One which were released about a year later. In January of 2017, the company stopped making the Wii U and released the Nintendo Switch in 2017. Since 2017, the company's stock price has steady increased to where it is today. There were many other consoles that were released that I didn't mention, but that is because there wasn't anything significant that I saw when looking at the chart. Not only do you want to know what the company has done, but you also want to know what its competitors have done. Although its listed in the "Electronics Gaming & Multimedia" sector, its early history almost appears cyclical, depending on the success of its newly released consoles. While I do think the company is undervalued and will be around for a long time (and I will add it to my watch list), it isn't something I would invest in for my particular strategy. There is simply too much competition, and while Nintendo is a great company, I already invest in Microsoft. Not only does Microsoft have an excellent gaming console, but they also have an insane amount of patents/products/services that puts them completely on a different level. Although they are in different sectors, I prefer companies that have many ways of generating income. Another stock I invest in is Meta because not only are they a social media giant, but they are also invested in VR. Both my wife and I have an Oculus Quest, and it is by far the best console I have ever owned. While I do believe the company is good and is undervalued, it isn't the investment for me.

To sum it up, identify great companies and their competition, make sure they have good performance and good financial health, find out what caused price fluctuations throughout their history (past and present), and do the same thing for their competitors. If the competitors do it better year after year, the chances of their competitors continuing that trend becomes more likely with each consecutive year. The reason I don't invest in them is because I'm invested in their competitors who perform better. From 2013 to 2023, Nintendo had a compound annual growth rate (CAGR) of 16.42%, Microsoft with 29.53%, and Meta with 26.52%. As a benchmark, the S&P 500 had a 13.59% CAGR during the same period. Like I said, it's a good company, but it's not one I will invest in based off my investment strategy.

Balance sheet

Simply put, a balance sheet is a snapshot of the company's financial health over a certain period, and it's essentially a report of the company's financial worth. It is broken down into three main parts: assets, liabilities, and equity. It is called a balance sheet because all parts have to balance out (assets = liabilities + equity). The amount will be broken down into different categories in the three sections, and other companies will have different categories depending on their business type.

To simplify a balance sheet as much as possible, I will discuss the portions I look at when researching a company to help me conclude. The balance sheet has three main categories: assets, liabilities, and equity. Assets are what the company owns. Liabilities include everything the company owes, and the Equity section is the difference between the two (equity = assets - liabilities).

Each category gets broken down into subcategories that allow you to have a better understanding of that portion of the balance sheet. In the Asset column, you will see many line items, such as

- Cash or Cash & Cash Equivalents (cash available);
- Accounts receivable (money owed to the company but hasn't been paid yet [think of companies that have a store credit system]);
- Inventories (the monetary value of all inventory in stock);
- Total current assets (things that the company owns that can be easily converted to cash and sold within a year ["Current" on a balance sheet typically means within a twelve-month period]);
- Gross Property, Plant, & Equipment (the total value of land, buildings, manufacturing plants, equipment, machinery, and office equipment owned by the company);
- Less Accumulated Depreciation (depreciation over time of the "Gross Property, Plant, & Equipment" category; this is calculated by an IRS formula and is a tax deduction for the company);
- Net Property, Plant, & Equipment (Gross Property, Plant, & Equipment - Less Accumulated Depreciation); and
- Total Assets (this is the total of all assets).

In the Liabilities category, you will see line items such as

- Accounts Payable (money the company owes but hasn't paid yet [this could be things such as bills, insurance payments, etc.]);

- Bank Debt (money owed by the company to a bank/financial institution);
- Total Current Liabilities (liabilities owed within a twelve-month period);
- Long-Term Debt (debts owed that aren't due within a twelve-month period); and
- Total Liabilities (total of all liabilities).

In the Equities category, you will see line items such as

- Paid-in Capital (total amount invested into the company by an investor or new owner, or issued and sold stocks to an investor);
- Retained Earnings (monetary value that is being reinvested into the company's assets to grow the company in some aspect or other);
- Liabilities & Shareholder Equities (the difference between the assets and liabilities is considered the shareholders equity, but for this portion, it's Total Liabilities + Shareholders Equity);
- Shares Outstanding (number of shares in circulation); and
- Equity or Book value Per Share (book value is stockholder's equity divided by outstanding shares, and you can get the price to book ratio by dividing the current stock price by the book value).

It may seem like a lot of information at first, but it only takes a few minutes to go through, and most attention only goes to specific sections. Actually, there are only a few things that I do to evaluate a balance sheet (some investors go into a lot more depth, and some don't look at financial reports at all).

First, I look at the current ratio, which is one of the formulas a lender will use to determine whether or not they will lend money to a company. Lenders prefer a ratio between 1.2 and 2 and consider anything less than 1 to need a closer look, depending on what industry it's in. Specific industries utilize leverage to grow. To calculate the ratio, divide your total current assets by your total current liabilities. If the ratio is less than .8, I no longer consider that company for investment purposes. My reason is I invest in the technology industry, which tends to have a lower current ratio (this is based on the level of risk I'm willing to take, but if a bank isn't that willing to lend to them because the ratio is used to determine if a company can pay their bills, I'm less inclined to invest in it). Depending on your investment strategy, this may or may not be a tool you use to analyze the company. The fastest way to find it is to use Yahoo Finance on a mobile device, search for the company, scroll down to the "Key Statistics," and click "View More." This will give you a quick look at everything you need, and you will find the current ratio calculated for you near the bottom (in the Balance Sheet section).

If you like investing in growth companies that utilize leverage, the assets compared to liabilities may be slightly skewed. For growth companies specifically, make sure that the assets are growing more than the liabilities and that the earnings per share increases year after year.

If they pass this first evaluation, I look at their Cash & Cash Equivalents to see if it is greater, or at least equal to, their Current Liabilities (another check to ensure the company can pay their short-term bills). Again, depending on your investment strategy, this may vary or be irrelevant. You can use stock screeners to quickly search through every company within seconds.

As long as the first two evaluations show a relatively healthy company, I don't consider much else. The visual observation makes it easy to find highly successful companies, so a quick look to ensure they aren't drowning in debt is an assurance that they could be a good choice.

There are many other ways people look at balance sheets (some more in-depth and some not), but this works best for me and is the most straightforward. It also doesn't take too much time, so if a company passes these evaluations, I look at the income statement to see where the money is coming from and going to and the company's annual report on their plans to improve and grow. Like with the balance sheet, a few categories get broken down into many line items depending on the company and industry (specific industries will have more line items than others). Remember, this is just a basic explanation of what I look for, so figure out what investment strategy you want to use and determine the metrics best for that particular strategy.

INCOME STATEMENT

An income statement summarizes the company's financial activity over a certain period. It will let you know how much the company is receiving and all the expenses and costs associated with it. It will ultimately let you know if your company has gained or lost money during that period. These statements are critical for a company because they list where all the money goes. Just like when we discussed your budget and wrote down all your income and expenses so we can identify and reduce them, a company does the same thing. They evaluate the financial reports regularly because a company with poor financial management is doomed to failure. Companies like to compare their statement to the previous ones; they also compare them to their industry's average or other companies within the same industry.

You can do this from several websites, but I prefer to use Google. Then you can see how the company's income statement compares to that industry's average, so you can see if their liabilities and expenses are higher than the average or lower. You can compare their income versus expenses to see if the company is more or less efficient than the industry average. This can key you into whether that company is doing well or may run into trouble in the future. For example, companies can determine if they are paying more or less than the industry average for materials and labor. They can see how much they pay in salary as well.

When a business has a massive layoff, the company goes through its income statement to determine the best way to reduce its overall cost, which affects the company the least. You can only cut down the cost of materials so much before your products have a lower quality and you have control over the cost of freight if you find another company to work with. Not all companies pay into research and development, but the ones who do have to have an edge on their competitor or they will ultimately be passed over.

This leaves them with the options of the things they can control that have the most negligible impact on the company, which is why layoffs are sometimes necessary for a company to survive. For every job lost, however, hundreds of jobs are created because of all the new companies created yearly (they don't get the media's attention, so you never hear about the latest jobs available).

Let's go through the main parts of an income statement without further delay and provide a simple definition:

- Sales revenue—all income generated from the company's goods and services
- Interest income—interest that is generated from savings accounts, investment accounts, government bonds, or interest for money that was loaned to another company or institution
- Net revenue—sales revenue + interest income
- Materials and manufacturing labor—cost of all materials, manufacturing, and the cost of labor for those things
- Selling, general, and administrative (SG&A)—essentially the cost of operating and promoting the product
- Research and development expense—monetary value spent toward research and development for future products and the improvement of current ones
- Depreciation—just as with your balance sheet, depreciation is the decrease in value over time for things like equipment, machinery, buildings, plants, and company vehicles. The formulas used come from the IRS and this deduction is done by the financial department of a company and counts as a tax deduction.
- Interest expense—any interest the company has paid toward a loan, debt, or another company for the use of borrowed money

- Total cost—materials and manufacturing labor + selling, general, and administrative + research and development expense + depreciation + interest expense
- Earnings before federal and state taxes—income received before paying taxes
- Taxes—amount of income paid to taxes
- Net income—gross income - expenses and taxes
- Shares outstanding—the number of shares in circulation
- Income per share—the amount of money the company is earning per each share

While there is a lot of information on the income statement, the majority is used for the company to make better decisions to improve the company. It's essential to know how a company makes money, and it's important to understand how much it makes compared to how much it spends. While it also may appear overwhelming, there are only a few things that I focus on when researching a company's income statement.

- First, I take the company's income statement and convert it to a percentage by dividing each line item by net sales. This will allow me to compare it to the industry average for the company or other companies in the same industry.
- After converting to percentages, I compare their sales revenue to previous reports to look for increased revenue.
- Then I look at their expenses and see if they have increased or decreased. I love to know when a company is reducing its costs because it shows it is actively improving its financial health. Many fast-growing companies are highly leveraged with a lot of long-term debt, so it is essential to see where the money comes from and what it's going toward.
- Next, I look to see if their net income has increased.
- Finally, I look at their earnings per share to evaluate the company's growth. The earnings per share is calculated by dividing the company's earnings by the number of shares outstanding. It can be found at the bottom of the income

statement. Earnings per share (EPS) is probably one of the more critical things to consider when looking for fast-growing companies. If their EPS has increased each year for the last five years, it is typically a safe assumption that it will continue to rise for the next five years.

Peter Lynch usually talks about finding a company whose growth is higher than its P/E ratio (price/earnings ratio = stock current price divided by annual earnings) because they are considered undervalued. He states that you should expect the P/E ratio to be around the same as their growth, and if you find one with higher growth and a lower P/E ratio, you find yourself a bargain. He ran a fund and was constantly looking for stock selling for a price well below what it should be, and he has an amazing track record to show that it works. I don't use this method, but I did want to share it because I believe it is a great technique for finding undervalued companies and leads to amazing gains. Because of my work schedule, I needed an investment strategy that didn't require me to research new companies constantly. That is why I focus on identifying high-quality companies with a few ETFs that would ultimately give me a portfolio that is perfect for buying and holding those companies for a very long time. My actual portfolio only requires a few hours a year to maintain.

Summary of balance sheets and income statements

I plan to explain this in an easily understood and applied way. I explained the significant points of each document and the process I went through to help me decide which companies I would invest in. Here is a quick summary of each document. I recommend you review several companies' documents to start getting practice. If it helps, print out one of each, go through it with a highlighter, and post it near your computer so it becomes second nature when you do this in the future. You will no longer need visual guidance after spending a few months putting it into practice. To make it even easier for you, you can download Yahoo Finance on your phone or use your computer, and you can find both of these documents as well as the cash flow statement.

BALANCE SHEET EVALUATION SUMMARY

- Use the current ratio to determine if a lender would consider it safe to issue a loan to and learn the average for the industry the particular company is in. Compare these two and try to understand what the reason is. Some companies are highly leveraged, so their current ratio will be much lower than companies who aren't trying to expand as rapidly.
- Check to see if cash and cash equivalents are greater to, or at least equal to, the current liabilities.
- Utilizing visual observation and then verifying a good financial foundation is a great way to reduce the risk of investing in poor companies.

INCOME STATEMENT EVALUATION SUMMARY

- Convert each line item to a percentage by dividing it by net sales, then use a website to compare each line item to the industry's average or other companies in the same industry (you can also Google it as there are so many websites and businesses dedicated to researching companies, most of the work will more than likely already be done for you).
- Look for an increase in sales revenue from their previous reports then compare to the industry average.
- Check to see if the expenses for the company have been increasing or decreasing compared to previous statements then compare to the industry average.
- Check to see if net income has been increasing compared to their previous reports and then to the industry average.

- Check to make sure that earnings per share has continued to increase on each report and then compare to the industry average (if you are searching for growth investments, earnings per share is one of the more important metrics people look at).

Now that we have reviewed the information, it's time to narrow your list further. Remember in the "Asset Allocation" section when I told you that I considered investing in bonds to be good advice that many high-profile fund managers and investors recommend. Still I stated that I didn't follow that advice and would say why later. Well, this is why. Stocks have historically outperformed bonds by more than double. While bonds are considered safe in that they can keep you from losing value in a bad market, they also prevent you from the average returns you would get by investing in stocks instead.

Part of the reason is that I'm investing for the long term (greater than twenty years). Because I utilize dollar-cost averaging, I plan to continue investing no matter how bad the market or how low prices become. No matter how bad the market has gotten, it has always recovered from its losses and continued to rise. Because I'm on a long investment timeline, I intend to use that time as efficiently as possible by investing in high-quality growth companies to benefit from the capital appreciation. Usually, when people get older, they tend to assign more of their portfolio to bonds because of the safe and guaranteed returns (even if it doesn't beat inflation, which is one of the primary reasons I decided to stay away from them for now).

One thing I have noticed, and some other fund managers and investors have mentioned in several interviews, is that even when the market is terrible, not all companies and industries are affected the same way. You saw this during the COVID-19 pandemic in stores like Walmart and Costco (toilet paper and infant formula supplies remained the same, but the demand increased drastically [because of fear and panic], causing a nationwide shortage). You did very well in comparison to companies in other industries. Companies that produce consumer products do well when the market is up and significant when the market is down compared to other companies.

Regardless of how bad things get, a few things are certain. Everyone needs to eat, shower (hopefully, we can all agree), shave, dress, commute to work/store, etc. A company that provides products needed for everyday use tends to perform better during recessions and global pandemics. Stores like Costco do great because, with inflation, the cost of goods increases, so they adjust the price to match, and people need to eat. Another reason Costco is an excellent company for investing is because statistics have shown that most of their consumer base is the upper-middle class and the upper class (this is important because these classes are more financially responsible [how they got there in the first place]; hence, they aren't as negatively impacted by these events and continue shopping at the store).

Instead of investing in bonds to protect from inflation, I prefer investing in companies that do great in a bad market and decent in a good market, especially those that pay dividends. While I have yet to talk about companies paying dividends in this book, they typically have more cash available than they can put to use, so they spend a specific portion out yearly to shareholders as a reward for owning the stock. The companies that do this are usually large, and many have increased their dividend payout annually. They even have categories—like dividend kings, dividend aristocrats, dividend achievers, etc.—that have increased their dividends every year for a certain amount of time (each category is for a certain amount of time, among other requirements). Having dividend-paying companies in your portfolio is a great thing to do and something I do for myself and encourage others to do. Some people's investment strategy involves only investing in dividend-paying companies and reinvesting the dividend payouts to accelerate the growth of their portfolio along with the capital appreciation they receive. There are even dividend-focused ETFs and index funds (SCHD is another one from Charles Schwab that does well but is dividend-focused).

As I mentioned, there are thousands of different investment strategies, and all of them have pros and cons compared to others. Instead of bonds, I stick with stocks that perform well during recessions and/or pay dividends to benefit from the growth and protection from inflation. As I get older, I will eventually start moving my investments into slower-growing dividend-paying companies (dividend payments are taxable income and usually paid quarterly), so when I'm ready to retire, I will receive payments every year from my dividends without having to sell my stock and enough growth through my portfolio selection to continue to grow my investments.

The growth that I have over time will allow me to have a fantastic dividend payout to live off of (not to mention my 401(k) and Social Security or the income I'll be receiving from rental properties [which you will learn out to do in the next chapter], royalties from the books that I write, or the income for the businesses I plan to start) while continuing to grow my portfolio. When it is my time to leave this world, I will be able to leave my family with multiple forms of passive income that can provide for them for many generations to come.

This is what I want to happen for you and your family. I want you to be able to change your life and start living the life you deserve. I started off my adult life in the lower class and brutally and painfully made my way through the middle class until I finally reached the upper class. It was a long and challenging journey for my family and me. Still, I devoted a lot of time and resources to learning what I needed to do and the changes I had to make to improve my life. My journey to get out of debt led me to work three different jobs to earn a six-figure income to pay off debt as quickly as possible, and after paying off my debt, I was able to switch to only one job that not only paid a six-figure income, but it also paid more than the previous three combined. If you are still reading this book (only 20 percent of people read through an entire book), it means that you genuinely want to change your life and have already taken steps in the right direction. The only thing more important than learning what to do is actually applying what you learned and doing it. Knowledge is power *only* if used, so keep that in mind as you finish reading this book.

Reread this book as often as needed to help you succeed or better understand it. Research other ways to increase your income, reduce expenses, and invest your income. Never stop growing or trying to improve. Invest in your education and in the education of your spouse and children but know that college isn't the only source of education. You are only limited by the limits you place on yourself.

If you are starting your journey in the lower class like I did, use that as motivation to improve your situation and climb the ranks. If you are beginning your journey in the middle class, be thankful you have a better starting position. Use that to motivate you as you improve your situation and climb the ranks. Suppose you are already in the upper class and are reading this book, in that case, you need to understand that the most significant difference between the lower, middle, and upper classes is the financial situation we are born into and the financial decisions we make afterward. If you are born into a family with poor financial management, you will likely do the same things they did. Use that information to help you understand people's struggles and what they need to change their situation. Use it to motivate you to share your knowledge with others and to help those around you. It doesn't matter where your journey begins but the path you take to change your situation. Everyone wants to be happy and prosperous by whatever measures they use to define those terms. Help each other learn and grow; together, we can give this world a better future.

If anything you have learned from this book has helped you, please let me know by leaving a review and contacting me at jeff.shannon32@yahoo.com because the reviews will help me reach more people. The emails will allow me to talk with the people I was able to help make a difference. Again, I'm swamped, and depending on how many emails I receive, it may take a while for them to get to you. But I promise I will try my best to respond to everyone who reaches out with questions, needs advice, or wants to say thank you.

CREATING YOUR PORTFOLIO

You can set up your portfolio in endless ways, and personal preference can play a significant role. Another essential factor would be which platform you are going to use. A portfolio that is right for me may not be suitable for you. If you want ETFs that track companies with growth, for example, two good options are the Schwab US Large-Cap Growth ETF (SCHG) and the Vanguard Growth ETF (VUG). SCHG has an average annual return of 15 percent (its five-year return is 93.1 percent and its YTD is 35.13 percent), and VUG has an average yearly return of 14 percent (its five-year return is 93.1 percent and its YTD is 35.13 percent). These are two ETFs on two different platforms tracking similar things and diversified between 250-ish companies (and those companies are all part of the S&P 500). These spread out your risk and puts out average returns that perform better than the average market. If you decide to invest in index funds, you can still have diversification and lower fees. Some platforms don't allow fractional shares (owning a fraction of a share) or dividend reinvestment programs (DRIP), which may affect your decision. If I had chosen to invest in index funds, I would use Warren Buffet's suggestion and choose one that tracks the S&P. As for the one for my securities/bond, I would choose one that follows Treasury Inflation-Protected Securities (also known as TIPS). If inflation goes up, the value goes up, which protects you from losing money from inflation.

If you are new to investing, it is best to stick with investing in ETFs or index funds. As I said earlier, the diversity it brings to your portfolio already helps to protect your investments and will allow you to grow your portfolio continuously. I'm not a financial advisor and can't recommend which stocks you should invest in, but I will talk about multiple platforms and provide a few examples of different kinds of ETFs. The purpose is to give an example to help you get started. Always do your own research before making any investment decision.

PORTFOLIO EXAMPLES FROM DIFFERENT PLATFORMS

Below, I will list five different apps you can use to start invest-ing. My favorite app (M1 Finance) is more complicated to set up initially. Still automating your investments is fantastic once it is set up. It also has built-in portfolios you can choose from if you want to use them instead of making your own, which is excellent for people new to investing.

Listed below are the five apps I will briefly discuss:

- M1 Finance
- Robinhood
- Webull
- eToro
- Acorns

Before I begin discussing the apps, I would like to give you a list of different ETFs for you to consider when building your starting portfolio, and I will also provide an example from the ones I give you as well as the different ratios to show how the growth and dividend percentage changes. The examples I will provide for you outperform the S&P 500 year after year, but I will also provide more to help get you started.

ETF COMBINATIONS THAT BEAT THE S&P's PERFORMANCE

Four growth ETFs to consider

Growth ETFs are great for a portfolio because they focus on companies that continue to grow year after year. For long-term investing, these are excellent options as most tend to outperform the S&P 500 (all the ones I listed do). Although they come with a little more risk, they are still diversified among many other growth stocks which reduces your overall risks while still giving you more gains than the S&P. I personally prefer holding a growth ETF as opposed to one that tracks the S&P as it gives consistently better returns.

1. VUG—Vanguard Growth Index Fund currently has a holding of 221 companies (compared to the S&P's 500 holdings) with a focus on large-cap growth stocks with a

ten-year average annual return of 13.97 percent. Its three largest holdings are Apple at 13 percent, Microsoft at 12.77 percent, and Amazon at 6.46 percent. Out of the three growth ETFs I will mention, this one has the lowest average annual growth around 15 percent, but it is also more diversified and stable overall. It has an expense ratio of .04 percent.

2. SCHG—Schwab US Large-Cap Growth ETF currently has a holding of 252 companies (compared to the S&P's 500 holdings) with a focus on large-cap growth stocks with a ten-year average annual return of 14.88 percent, and it regularly outperforms the S&P500. It has 43.89 percent of its holdings in technology companies, such as Apple and Microsoft, and technology is one of the fastest growing industries there is. Its current tech holdings make up 46.51 percent, with communication services coming in second at 12.68 percent. It has an expense ratio of .04 percent.

3. QQQM—Invesco NASDAQ 100 ETF currently has a holding of 103 companies (less than half of QQQM) with a focus on large-cap growth with 49.87 percent in information technologies. Apple, Microsoft, and Amazon are their three biggest holdings at 8.96 percent for Microsoft, 8.79 percent for Apple, and 4.85 percent for Amazon. Its ten-year average annual return is 17.65 percent. It has an expense ratio of .15 percent.

4. VGT—Vanguard Information Technology ETF currently has a holding of 314 companies (the most out of the 4 ETFs mentioned in this section), with technology companies making up 99.34 percent of the portfolio with its ten-year average return of 19.65 percent. Apple makes up 21.49 percent while Microsoft makes up 19.77 percent. It has an expense ratio of .10 percent.

These are the top four growth ETFs in my opinion, but the one you choose should depend on your risk tolerance. I listed them in order from the lowest ten-year average to the highest, and the risk increases as you go down. All these have outperformed the S&P 500, so I tend to group them into two categories. Many people prefer investing into a fund that tracks the S&P 500, but in my opinion, using VUG or SCHG instead would give you better returns. The reason is because the biggest drivers of the S&P 500's growth come from six specific companies, which are Apple, Microsoft, Amazon, Netflix, Google, and Meta. If you take these out of the S&P 500, the average of the remaining 494 holdings are almost insignificant.

Those companies are the reason these four growth ETFs perform so well and something you need to consider. The opposite of diversity when it comes to investing is having a strong focus in a particular industry or sector. These growth ETFs are less diverse and have their largest holdings in the technology.

Four index funds that track growth

1. MGK—Vanguard Mega Cap Growth Index Fund: It has an expense ratio of .07 percent and a ten-year annualized return of 14.7 percent.
2. SWLGX—Schwab US Large-Cap Growth Index Fund: It has an expense ratio of .035 percent, and its five-year annualized return is 14.16 percent (it was created in 2017, so a ten-year comparison isn't available at the time of this writing).
3. VIGAX—Vanguard Growth Index Fund Admiral Shares: It has an expense ratio of .05 percent and a ten-year annualized return of 12.88 percent.
4. FBGRX—Fidelity Blue Chip Growth Fund: It has an expense ratio of .69 percent and

Four ETFs that track the S&P 500

1. SPY—SPDR S&P 500 ETF Trust: It has an expense ratio of .095 percent with high daily trade volume. Its ten-year annualized returns at the time of writing this is 11.93 percent.

2. IVV—iShares Core S&P 500 ETF: It has an expense ratio of .03 percent although it has no small-cap equity exposure and has a higher concentration of the technology sector. Its ten-year annualized returns of 12 percent.

3. VOO—Vanguard S&P 500 ETF: Essentially the ETF version of Vanguard's index mutual fund VFIAX (which is known for having low fees). It has an expense ratio of .03 percent and is the ETF most people think of when you mention the S&P 500. Its ten-year annualized return is 11.99 percent.

4. SPLG—SPDR Portfolio S&P 500 ETF: Pretty much the same as SPY but with a lower expense of .02 percent. Its ten-year annualized return is 11.96 percent.

Four index funds that track the S&P 500

1. VFIAX—Vanguard 500 Index Fund Admiral Shares: It has an expense ratio of .04 percent and requires a minimum investment of $3,000. It has a ten-year annualized return of 10.10 percent.

2. SWPPX—Schwab S&P 500 Index Fund: It has an expense ratio of .02 percent and a ten-year annualized return of 11.97 percent.

3. FXAIX—Fidelity 500 Index Fund: It has an expense ratio of .015 percent and a ten-year annualized return of 12.6 percent.

4. FNILX—Fidelity Zero Large Cap Index: It has the lowest expense ratio, which is 0.00 percent. It also has a ten-year annualized return of 11.58 percent.

Four dividend ETFs to consider

1. VYM—Vanguard High Dividend Yield ETF: 3.12 percent dividend yield, 9.38 percent compound annual growth rate (with dividends reinvested), and 6 percent ten-year average CAGR without dividends reinvested. It has 450 holdings

in its portfolio, with its three largest positions being J.P. Morgan at 3.48 percent, Broadcom at 3.42 percent, and Exxon Mobil at 2.87 percent. Its largest weight is financial services, which make up 21.65 percent of the portfolio, followed by 13.43 percent in consumer defensive.

2. NOBL—ProShares S&P 500 Dividend Aristocrats ETF: 2.10 percent dividend yield, 10.14 percent ten-year CAGR (compound annual growth rate, with dividends reinvested), and 7.99 percent ten-year CAGR without dividends reinvested. It has sixty-eight holdings, with its top three being Franklin Resources at 1.78 percent, Sherwin-Williams at 1.78 percent, and Target at 1.75 percent. Its portfolio weighting has 23.29 percent in industrials and 22.92 percent in consumer defensive.

3. DGRO—iShares Core Dividend Growth ETF: 2.45 percent dividend yield, 10.81 percent ten-year average CAGR (with dividends reinvested), and 7.99 percent eight-year average CAGR without dividends reinvested (it's eight years because it came out in 2015, instead of ten-year average used for the rest). It has a total of 422 holdings, with its top three positions being J.P. Morgan at 2.97 percent, Microsoft at 2.92 percent, and Broadcom at 2.82 percent. Its portfolio weighting is 18.17 percent in financial services and 17.97 percent in technology.

4. SCHD—Schwab US Dividend Equity ETF: 3.49 percent dividend yield, 11.03 percent compound annual growth rate (with dividends reinvested), and 7.58 percent ten-year average CAGR without dividends reinvested. It has a total of 102 holdings, with its top three being Broadcom at 4.44 percent, AbbVie at 4.19 percent, and Home Depot at 4.17 percent. Its largest portfolio weightings are 17.14 percent industrials and 16.73 percent in financial services.

These are the top four dividend ETFs in my personal opinion. When it comes to dividend paying ETFs, it still comes down to personal preference, but the favorite of pretty much anyone who invests in dividends almost always add SCHD to their portfolio. Not only does it have good growth, but it also has a higher dividend yield than the others.

CREATING SIMPLE BUT GREAT-PERFORMING PORTFOLIOS

To give you simple portfolios that you can set and forget, it's important to consider your age and your retirement plans first. The younger you are, the more emphasis you want to put on growth. The older you are, the more you would want going in to dividends (or bonds if you choose to go that route). Dividend paying stocks essentially pay you dividends for owning the stock, and it's a great hedge against inflation. Having dividend-paying stocks that also have growth makes it even more impressive as you will benefit from capital appreciation and dividends. As I stated earlier, I don't invest in bonds because stocks have always outperformed them in the long run, so for my securities portion of my portfolio, I prefer investing in dividend stocks.

So let's use the ETFs listed above and start putting them together. The ratios we are going to use is 70/30, 60/40, 50/50, 40/60, and 30/70 with risk and securities respectively. The S&P 500 during this ten-year average is 13.59 percent CAGR with dividends reinvested and 11.62 percent without as a comparison.

The information is as follows:

- 70 percent QQQM and 30 percent SCHD—With dividends reinvested, its CAGR is 17.73 percent, and without dividends reinvested, its CAGR is 15.94 percent. It has a dividend yield of 1.48 percent.
- 60 percent QQQM and 40 percent SCHD—With dividends reinvested, its CAGR is 17.15 percent, and without dividends reinvested, its CAGR is 15.12 percent. It has a dividend yield of 1.77 percent.

- 50 percent QQQM and 50 percent SCHD—With dividends reinvested, its CAGR is 16.53 percent, and without dividends reinvested, its CAGR is 14.26 percent. It has a dividend yield of 2.05 percent.
- 40 percent QQQM and 60 percent SCHD—With dividends reinvested, its CAGR is 15.87 percent, and without dividends reinvested, its CAGR is 13.37 percent. It has a dividend yield of 2.34 percent.
- 30 percent QQQM and 70 percent SCHD—With dividends reinvested, its CAGR is 15.17 percent, and without dividends reinvested, its CAGR is 12.43 percent. It has a dividend yield of 2.63 percent.

By combining these two ETFs, you have diversification through many stocks, and it results in better growth than the S&P 500, and it has a better dividend yield as well. Since we are using SCHD for protection against inflation, you need to decide how much you want in risk and how much in growth. If you want to add a little more risk, you can switch out QQQM with VGT which has even more focus on technology, but if you would rather it be less risky, you can switch it for SCHG (or VUG, but the SCHG outperforms it regularly) to get essentially what I consider to be the best half of the S&P 500 (which means less dilution and better gains). All you have to do now is simply invest the same amount of money each month using dollar cost-averaging and let it grow. This style of investment is perfect for beginners or people too busy to do a lot of research into individual stocks. With this style of portfolio, you simply invest the same amount every month and rebalance annually. If you want to test out different portfolios before you start to invest, you can use the website Backtest Portfolio Asset Allocation (portfoliovisualizer.com) to back test your portfolio to see how it compares to others.

If you wanted to make a Warren Buffet-styled portfolio, I also provided a list of four index funds that track the S&P 500; however, every single bond I found had very poor performance, and that is because it was they are directly affected by interest rates and inflation. I would recommend replacing the bond section with a dividend ETF like SCHD because it has both growth and a decent yield and is made up of solid companies.

M1 Finance

M1 Finance is my app of choice because I love how I am able to automate my investing. With a simple click of a button, I can rebalance my portfolio. While I would highly recommend it to anyone interested in investing, it isn't exactly beginner-friendly. The first time I tried to set up my own "Pie" (investment portfolio), it took a long time before I figured out how to do it correctly. If it wasn't for the several YouTube videos I watched that walked me through it, I would have wasted a lot of time trying to figure it out on my own. They do have tutorials showing you how to set it up, but I found YouTube to be more helpful.

After setting it up, however, it became extremely easy and took all the stress out of investing and made everything very easy. Once I learned how to set things up, I can quickly create a new one within a few minutes. Before you decide to use this app, you should definitely read the reviews of this app compared to others. I found this amazing article written by June Sham on NerdWallet ("M1 Finance Review 2024: Pros, Cons and How It Compares") where you can read all about the app in depth as well as compare it to other apps that are available. Out of the ones she reviews, M1 actually has the lowest rating. The things that she mentioned where the app "fell short" was because you can't do option trading or invest in mutual funds, limited trading window, and a lack of educational resources.

For me, none of those are issues for me because I don't trade options and I would never invest in mutual funds because of the expensive fees, and the lack of educational resources on the app don't bother me at all. I prefer researching multiple sources to hopefully remove any biases and to get a different perspective. For long-term automated investing, this app is perfect for me. Check out the link and you can see the review of other apps and decide what is better for you. I would give this app a 5 out of 5 because it is exactly what

I wanted. If you are interested in using the same app, you can get it through this link https://m1.finance/yKFCnrv5Y4Zh or you can go to your App Store to download it. If you don't like the idea of a mobile app, you can also go to their website.

ROBINHOOD AND WEBULL

I don't use either of these, but I have read great things about them and know people who use them. While your investing isn't automated like with M1 Finance, they still are amazing and have many trading tools and indicators that many people love to use. These would be better options for those who swing trade or are active investors, so once you determine which style of investing is better for you, you should decide which app or brokerage works best for your needs.

eTORO

If you simply don't have the time or interest in learning and developing the skills required for investing in the stock market and/ or the cryptocurrency market or you don't have time to monitor the market and research companies, eToro is unique in that it has a patented copy trading technology which allows you to find and copy the trades of successful investors on the platform. It will essentially make the same trades as the investor you selected, and it allows you to see what they are doing in real-time. Not only will it automatically copy their trades in your own account, but you can also communicate with them to ask questions or to thank them. If you don't want to copy an investor, you can instead copy portfolios. "CopyPortfolios" will allow you to copy the portfolios of successful long-term investors that are using individual companies, ETFs and indexes, or a combination. Some of these are designed to follow specific companies, follow the market, or others that follow certain industries.

You are able to look through the successful investors statistics on their profiles to show you their gains and losses, and eToro assigns each trader a risk score between 1 and 10. A score of 1 is the lowest risk possible while the highest risk is 10. The score is determined by their past performance as well as market fluctuations among other things all rolled into an algorithm designed by the company to give a great representation of how much risk the portfolio will have. Being able to view their past performances and trades will give you great insight into their investing style, and you can also read posts they make as to why they made certain investment decisions.

To become an investor that others can copy, there are a lot of requirements that you have to meet which filters out a lot of investors with poor performances or not enough history on the platform. This is a great thing for you because the traders you are able to see have already met the minimum requirements, which leaves you with trying to find the one that works for you. To make it easier for you, eToro sets up different categories, such as Popular Investors which will allow you to see which ones have the most followers copying their trades. This can be a good indication because when you look at their statistics and see they are making great returns, you can look at how many followers they have. People will stick with them if they continue to make good investment decisions. You can also follow multiple traders, so if you ever decide the one you were with isn't working for you, you can simply switch to another investor. In 2020, while we were dealing with the pandemic, eToro's top fifty copied traders had an average annual gain of 83.7 percent. They are the most copied traders for a reason.

When you become a successful investor yourself and you trade from their platform, you can eventually earn your spot at becoming a trader that others can copy, and depending on your performances and number of people copying your trades, the company will pay you. You could turn your investments into an additional stream of passive income by having people copy your trades. Not only will your money be growing just from your normal investments, but you will also be paid for it!

I believe it is best to find a trader who invests for long-term growth because they tend to invest in high-quality companies that are leaders in their industry that continues to create products, patents, and/services that are in demand, which keeps them ahead of their competition. I also believe the company they are investing in should be growing every year and increasing their profits while having little debt. Certain industries have different average growth rates which will vary your expected returns, but my favorite industries to invest in are technology, real estate, energy, and financial. Before selecting a trader to copy, find one that has a level of risk you are comfortable with, invests in companies or industries you are familiar with, and plan on holding those companies for at least five years and also has a proven track record on his/her profile. This will help you find a good trader and give you a great outcome.

Acorns

This platform is one that I used at the very beginning of my journey. That is because of the feature they have where it invests your "change" by rounding up to the nearest dollar amount and investing it in an ETF (you can select to double the amount of your change or many other options). If you spend a $1.75 on a candy bar at the gas station and later that night order pizza for $26.67, the app will invest $0.25 into an ETF from the first purchase and $0.33 from the second one. Every time you spend money, the app will automatically invest the change for you without you having to think about it. If you are someone who gets a coffee every morning from Starbucks or gets their daily energy drinks from 7-Eleven, this app will be beneficial by investing spare change that you wouldn't have otherwise invested into an ETF. As for the ETFs to choose from, they are based off the amount of risk you are willing to take on. I recommend using their highest-risk ETF simply because it is so diversified; it is low risk but has better returns than the other options. If you consider inflation, you want your returns to at least beat inflation so you aren't losing money.

I haven't used Acorns in a while, and there are several reasons for this. The first reason is because I only use my debit card for ATM withdrawals. Once I learned how to use credit cards correctly, I strictly use credit cards for every purchase because of the rewards it provides. The second reason is while the app has a lot of features worth mentioning, it also has high fees that might make you want to use another platform entirely. When you are new to investing, you don't really pay attention to the fees associated with it or assume that it is just a part of the process. It wasn't until I began not only researching companies to invest in but also the different platforms I use when I discovered I was paying too much. Remember when I told you about compounding interest? Well, when you are paying fees, the money spent on them instead of your stocks can be looked at as if they were compounding losses. That is a big reason why Warren Buffet and others recommend index funds as they have the lowest fees and typically outperform mutual fund managers regularly.

As an example, you can use an app like Robinhood and invest into a specific ETF of your choice that easily outperforms the ones on Acorns without having the expensive fees. While some people may say that it's only a few dollars a month, they are forgetting what that amount can do when compounded over time. If you don't remember, check out the two examples I gave you earlier. You are essentially losing thousands in potential earnings to fees.

While I would rather invest using another platform with lower fees and more control over my investment, the round-up feature alone is the reason why many people still choose to use it (and many don't realize how much they lose to fees or they simply don't care). Only you know your financial situation, and if saving anything at all is very hard for you, this may be a good option. If you wanted to mimic the app, use a commission-free app like Robinhood and invest a dollar every time you spend money. If you don't feel like you have the funds or the discipline to start investing now, this may be a great option for you. If you like the idea of automatically having your change invested that doesn't require any thought or actions, this may be a great option for you. Everyone has a different opinion when it comes to the platform they prefer, so I recommend going on YouTube and checking out the experience and reviews of users of each platform.

REBALANCING YOUR PORTFOLIO

To rebalance, there are a few options. Some apps will allow you to set up percentages into how much of your payment goes into which stock (M1 Finance does this). Some also have a rebalance feature that can do it for you (M1 Finance has this option). If you are doing it manually, it is still relatively easy to do, and the lesser number of investment holdings you have, the easier. If you decided to invest in either ETFs or index funds like Warren Buffet and other high-profile investors suggested, you can invest in one that tracks the market or a specific part of the market for your risk/growth portion of your portfolio and another that tracks US Treasury bonds that are inflation-protected securities. If you did this, you would only have two to three ETFs or indexes in your portfolio (even if they track hundreds of companies). Let's say your portfolio contained two ETFs with 70 percent into risk/growth and 30 percent into securities/bonds with total of $100,000 total invested. This would mean that 70 percent of your total is $70,000 invested in risk/growth and $30,000 invested in securities/bonds. After a year, your portfolio did well and grew to a total of $113,400, but now your risk/growth makes up 82 percent of your portfolio ($92,988) and your securities/bond is only 18 percent of your portfolio ($20,412).

If this happens, you need to sell some of your risk/growth investment and invest it into your securities/bond investment. If you multiplied your total investment ($113,400) by .7 (70 percent), you can see that your risk growth total should be $79,380. If you take the $92,988 and subtract the $79,380, you are left with $13,608 (which is how much of your risk/growth needs to be sold and reinvested into your securities to return it to your predetermined ratios). If the stock you are invested in cost $50 per share, you can divide the amount you need to sell (in this example, $13,608) by the cost per share. So you would divide the $13,608 by $50 which gives you 680.4 shares you need to sell. Once it is sold, you would invest $13,608 into your securities/bond investments. This will get your portfolio back into balance, so you aren't taking on too much risk. Depending on how far from your original percentages your portfolio becomes, you may rebalance it quarterly, semiannually, or annually. I prefer doing it only once a year unless the portfolio changes drastically since the more often you buy/sell, the more you pay in fees and taxes.

QUICK SUMMARY

You now know that when you start investing, you want to allocate a certain amount to be invested every month using dollar-cost averaging. You also know how you can set aside a certain amount per month to improve the benefits of dollar-cost averaging. You learned that your portfolio should be a mixture of risk/growth and securities/ bond based off how much risk you are willing to accept, and you learned how to rebalance your portfolio to make sure your percentages stay the same to protect your investments. Now you need to figure out what you want to put into your risk/growth section and your securities/bond section. The options available depend on what platform you are using, but all platforms have premade portfolios if you don't want to create your own.

CHAPTER 8

INVESTING IN TAX LIEN CERTIFICATES AND TAX DEEDS

WHAT IS A TAX LIEN CERTIFICATE?

Some people may still be uncomfortable when it comes to investing in the stock market, and that is why I'm talking about multiple investing options in this book. Some have heard horror stories about market crashes throughout history or might have had family members who lost most of it. The unfortunate part was that if people kept their money in stocks after those crashes, they would have regained everything they had originally lost and then more. The stock market is up more than 70 percent of the time, but when it starts to trend downward, people panic and then sell while in a losing position. Even though the market has always recovered, the fear of losing causes enough people to stay away from the market altogether. For that reason, I decided to find other investment strategies to help those people. That is the people this chapter will probably help the most. This is a government-backed investment strategy that can provide great returns **(the returns vary from state to state)** that can allow you to invest without any risk.

TLCs and tax deeds are the only things mentioned in the book that I don't have direct experience with. I have also asked many people I know, and no one knew about them either. That was when I decided to look into them to find out what they truly were and how much of a risk they represent. After going through several books and many websites, I decided it would be a great addition to this book simply for the reason that a lot of people don't feel safe investing in stocks. This could be another option for you to consider, but as with any decision you make in life, do your own research. Each state has a different rate that it charges, so your returns will be different depending on where you live.

This may be something you haven't heard of, but is an option in many of the states within the US and can provide a higher return than the stock market average **(depending on where you live)**. To briefly explain what a tax lien certificate **(TLC)** is, it is a government lien on the real estate because of property owners failing to pay their property taxes on time. The cities use the money received from property taxes to fund government-ran facilities, such as police stations and firefighting stations, as well as taking care of the roads and parks in your city. Many of these cities have anywhere from several hundred thousand to millions in outstanding property taxes that are owed to them, so TLC states will allow the counties to hold tax lien auctions to sell the tax lien certificates to potential investors **(which would be you)**.

If you purchase a TLC, you are giving the government the property tax that is owed so they can use it for what they need immediately, and in return the government gives you all the fees, penalties, and interest that is charged to the person who failed to pay it on time. In Texas **(where I am from)**, you will get charged a 25 percent fee if you are late in paying your property taxes **(each state is different as to the percentage of the fees and penalties)**. Those fees and penalties will get paid to the TLC investor, meaning you can get guaranteed returns that are backed by the government. When the property owner pays the taxes, the state gives you back what you invested plus all the fees and penalties that accumulated. If they fail to pay their property taxes, you are essentially given the property as the government has a lien on the real estate that you purchased when buying the TLC.

Benefits of TLCs

Regardless of whether they pay or not, it benefits you. If they do pay back the taxes and all the penalties and fees, you get guaranteed returns. If they fail to pay the property taxes, you will essentially own the property for the cost of the taxes and fees that were owed. You can then keep the property and use it for your own investment purposes or you can sell the property for profit.

For people who don't feel comfortable investing in the stock market, this can be a great option for you because it is backed by the government. Depending on your state, it can be a very profitable investment. Since many people have never heard of tax lien certificates, there will be many times when you show up and you're the only one there to bid for them. In chapter 7, I talk about investing in stocks and chapter 9 talks about investing in real estate. I recommend you investing in all three of them if this is an option in your state.

Each county will hold the auctions at different times, so check with your local counties and other counties in your area. Even if you don't plan on investing yet, go to an auction so you can see it in action. If someone there is making a bid, ask them questions **(if they say it is okay)** and listen to their experiences. Many people travel to different auctions and invest, and some even do it full time. All the information you need will be provided to you before making the purchase so you know exactly what you are getting. This may be one of the safest investments you can make. If you are investing in stocks but don't want to invest in bonds because of the lower returns but you still want a way to protect your investments, you can invest in both stocks and TLCs to have guaranteed returns to go along with the stocks in your portfolio. There isn't a lot to TLCs, so this is a very short chapter. This will be a good option for those who don't feel comfortable investing in stocks.

INVESTING IN TAX DEEDS

The states that don't auction TLCs are considered deed states, which also hold auctions. These auctions aren't for the property tax lien like TLCs, but they auction the right of ownership for the properties. This means that you can purchase a home for a fraction of the cost **(essentially you are paying back taxes on the property, and as a result, you are given the deed to the property by the government)**, and it will be mortgage and lien-free **(some states will allow a property to be sold with the lien still attached to the property, so check with your state)**.

If you live in a deed state, it can be a great way to earn income as you can either sell the properties for profit, rent them out for passive income, or live in it yourself. I was going to put this in the next chapter which goes over real estate investing, but because of the similarities of TLC/tax deed auctions, I wanted to group them together. All the information needed on the properties will be available at the auction, so you will know exactly what you are getting. If you live on the border between states and one is a tax lien state and the other a deed state, take advantage of both options. They are both safe investments with a lot of benefits.

CHAPTER 9

INVESTING IN REAL ESTATE

Just like with stocks, there are many different ways to invest in real estate. In chapter 5, I talked about how to use your own property to generate income. If you don't have a house at the moment, this chapter can help you get started. While some real estate investors do it as a full-time job, I want to try and provide the easiest and safest way for you to start investing in real estate and easing your way into becoming a full-time investor if that is what you desire. This method will reduce the risk you face if the housing market crashes like it did in 2007–2008 and reduce the chances of being spread too thin. If the house is vacant, you still need to be able to cover all expenses. The method I share will let you start investing in real estate slower than most methods, but as time goes on, you will be able to buy properties at a much faster rate.

As stated in chapter 5, you can actually earn more income by renting rooms to roommates than renting out the entire house. I would recommend continuing this strategy because not only will you be able to live in your house for free, but it will also have positive cash flow and will be able to pay a much lower down payment (20–30 percent if you're using it as a rental investment or 3.5 percent with an FHA loan if it will be your primary residence for at least one year). When you first start looking for a house, keep in mind that your credit score is a determining factor as to what interest rate you will be paying. If you are working on building your credit now, you can still get a house, but the interest might be higher.

MORTGAGES

When it comes to mortgages and other loans, the beginning of the loan will have a much higher interest rate compared to principal. As an example, I will use a $200,000 home with an annual interest rate of 5 percent on a thirty-year loan.

This would be a monthly payment of $1,073.64, with $833.33 going toward interest and $240.31 going toward principle. The amount of interest you pay each month will go down slightly and the amount toward principle will increase slightly as a result. If you only make the minimum payments on your home, you will end up paying around 2.5 times (depending on the interest rate and term of the loan) the cost of the home during that thirty-year period. In this specific example, you will end up with you paying $386,511.57 (that's $186,511.57 in interest!) or almost 93 percent of the principal of your loan in interest.

Using this same example, just by paying an additional $1,000 a month toward principal would have the home paid off in 10.3 years (paying $56,311.19 in interest). Most people truly don't understand how much money they are actually paying over time, which makes this information even more essential to understand. What you are about to read are different real estate investing methods you can use, that will not only increase your income, but also allow you to pay off your properties very quickly. I will provide two different strategies for two kinds of people, but I recommend utilizing both methods eventually.

The strategies I recommend will save you a lot of money throughout your lifetime and is safe regardless of the market. Not only will it save you money, but it will also make you money which can be used to purchase more property or pay off properties. The two types of properties I recommend considering for these methods are single-family and multifamily homes (four units maximum). If later you decide you want to grow beyond and start investing into commercial properties, I recommend you doing your research prior to starting as well as finding a mentor (someone with actual experience in doing what you want to do) to give yourself the best chance of success.

SINGLE-FAMILY HOMES

If you choose a single-family home, you need to consider how many rooms you want to rent out, if there is enough parking to accommodate, if the house requires any maintenance (I think it's better to start with a house without many problems), and the size of the house. Based on the average cost of a one-bedroom apartment in the area where the house is located, you can use the numbers I provided in chapter 5 to figure out how much to charge per room. You can call a lender and ask for the average interest rate and use a mortgage calculator to find out an estimate as to what your mortgage payment would be. Ideally, the amount you earn in rent should be a decent amount higher than your mortgage. This will allow you to live in your house for free. Consider figuring out how many rooms you will rent and for what price to make sure it is more than the mortgage before deciding to purchase.

Remember, the location is important. If you are closer to a college, there will always be college students needing a place to live. If you get a house near a business district, there will always be people looking for a shorter commute to work. If you live near a theme park or amusement park, there will always be tourist looking for a short-term stay (perfect for Airbnb). Don't think of this property as your dream property but as a nice place to live. Later on, you will acquire nicer and better properties.

Since you will be living in the property as your primary residence for at least one year, you can get an FHA loan that only requires 3.5 percent down payment. If you have enough for a down payment, you are good to get a house (I recommend having $5,000 extra to pay for the inspection and closing costs as you may have to pay depending on if it's a buyers or sellers' market [and you definitely want to do an inspection]). If not, start saving in preparation of getting one. Try to get the longest term possible (thirty years is typically the longest, but after COVID-19, some lenders offered forty-year loans).

Once you are living in your house, use the steps in chapter 5 to find roommates. You should be earning more than your mortgage by a decent amount. What you need to do now is to use the income renting rooms brings you and pay the minimum monthly payment. I recommend waiting a week or two and calling the lender and request to make a payment toward principal only. I would recommend paying as much as you can, but make sure you are setting aside income for other future plans like automatically investing in stocks. Try to at least pay the same amount as the mortgage payment when you make your extra payment toward principal, but the more you pay, the less you will pay overall in interest.

This will allow you to pay your house off extremely fast. Depending on your income and using the methods I mention in chapter 5, you could potentially pay off your home in three to seven years. The reason why I recommended getting a longer loan term was to give you a lower payment so you can utilize your cash flow to pay off your home. Once you have paid off half of your mortgage, I would recommend refinancing (some investors refinance earlier, but when you refinance, there are fees attached. By waiting, you will benefit from improving your credit score over time and possibly getting a lower rate as well as potentially reducing your mortgage payment by half).

At this point, start to look online at what price houses that are similar to yours are renting for in your area. It may be lower than what you get from roommates, but the goal is to get more properties over time. Because you refinanced and have a lower mortgage payment, you should be able to rent the home for a positive cash flow. If that is the case, start looking for other homes that meet the same criteria you used to find your first house. When you decide to go forward, you pay your down payment and move in.

You can now rent your first house to a family, and to make it simple for you, I recommend getting a property manager. They handle applications, talk to potential tenants, manage any issues that come up, work as a middleman if any repairs/services are needed, and show the property to your potential tenants. They typically will get 10 percent of the price you set for the property, so set your price to account for that. You can do it without a property manager, but having one will take most of the stress out of it so you can continue focusing on your future plans.

Now that your first property is being rented and your room-mates are essentially paying for your new property, here is what you should do. Pay the minimum amount on your new mortgage and continue focusing on paying down the first one. Once you have the first one completely paid off, you need to start focusing on paying down the second one. At this point, your income will have increased as the payments from the first property aren't going to a mortgage and is now passive income going directly to you. You can allocate as much income as you can into your second property until you get the mortgage halfway paid off. Guess what you do after that? That's right, you refinance and start looking for another property.

This is where the game changes a little. Now you should start focusing on buying properties as an investment instead of your primary residence. That would require a 20–30 percent down payment depending on which lender you use (unless you purchase a multi-family home with the intent on living in one of the units to qualify for the 3.5 percent FHA loan), so start saving and start planning. You now have great cash flow between the two properties, and only one of them has a mortgage that other people are paying for. On a YouTube video from Dave Ramsey's podcast, he told a person who called in that ideally their mortgage payment on their home should only be 25 percent of their monthly income (this was their only home, not a rental investment). I like the advice he gives, but I think applying it to your rental properties would be a great safety net to prevent you from stretching too thin. What I mean by that is taking the total monthly mortgage payments from all your properties should be no greater than 25 percent of your income. The housing market crash of 2007–2008 is a perfect example because many investors were spread too thin by over-leveraging and couldn't make all the payments that were owed. It is better to be cautious than to be careless. Leverage is an amazing tool but can be dangerous if not used responsibly. I will talk about leverage later on.

If you keep the total monthly mortgage payments less than 25 percent of your income, you won't acquire properties as fast as other investors; however, your real estate investments are safe with great cash flow and you will pay them off sooner (saving hundreds of thousands from going toward interest). Many investors consider $200 to $300 per unit to be a good cash flow because the only money they put into it was the down payment they used as leverage. While it is a viable and lucrative method, it comes with a lot more risk. You may have less properties, but the cash flow from them will be significantly larger and the properties easier to manage. If you are renting your first property for $2,000 a month, you aren't losing most of it to the mortgage payment like most investors. Property taxes, property management fee, insurance, and repairs are the only expenses that would come out of this, so out of $2,000 a month, around $1,400 of it is straight profit from a single property (instead of a combined four to five properties with four to five times the headache that leveraging debt can have).

As you continue this cycle of rinse and repeat, you will acquire more properties at a faster rate. If you can keep the total mortgage payments below 25 percent of your income, you give yourself an amazing amount of protection. Another way to add an additional safety net is to create an emergency fund for each property using the same thing I mentioned in chapter 4. Take the total of your monthly expenses for that property and multiply by six. You will do this for each property by recording all monthly expenses on that property, such as the things I listed in the paragraph above. To make it even easier, set up a separate checking account for your property manager and keep your property's emergency fund in that account. If an emergency comes up, your property manager can access those funds to take care of it for you and provide the receipts later. This not only automates the process for you, but it makes it easier for the property manager since they don't have to try and get ahold of you right away.

MULTIFAMILY HOMES

The strategy with starting with a multifamily will be very similar to the single-family home, so I will keep this section shorter. On a single-family home, the number of bedrooms and bathrooms are important because they are typically rented by families who need the space. Multifamily homes are a little different as in the number of bedrooms and bathrooms aren't as important. For this method, you will be living in one of the units while renting out the others. You can still rent out to roommates if you have enough space to make it feasible, but it isn't required. These types of properties are duplexes, triplexes, and fourplexes.

Location is the most important thing, but you still want to make sure there is adequate parking available. The price of a multifamily home is usually higher than a single-family home, but because you will be living in one of the units, you will still be able to get an FHA loan requiring only a 3.5 percent down payment. To simplify the process, I would recommend getting a property manager to manage the other units. The simpler it is, the less stress there is for you. A 10 percent property fee is worth all the things they deal with for you. Because each unit is separate, you can rent each for the average price for your area, and if you have a triplex or fourplex, you can get a decent amount of cash flow coming in. With more units, however, there will be more chances for problems so be prepared.

Use the same strategy of paying down half of the mortgage and then refinancing. Afterward, search for another multifamily property to invest in. To get the 3.5 percent FHA loan down payment instead of 20 percent, you need to move into the new multifamily home (allow your property manager to take over the unit you were staying in). Rent out the other units and continue to pay off the first one while the renters pay for the other one. Once it's paid off, start paying off the other and refinance when the mortgage is halfway paid down.

Continue this cycle while trying to keep the total mortgage payments between all properties below 25 percent of your income. This is what keeps your investments safe. Feel free to use a combination of single and multifamily homes, just make sure that you have an emergency fund set aside for each property as you go. This protects both you and your assets.

How to leverage debt to benefit you

If you have a home that you have been making payments on for a while, you probably have a lot of equity available for leverage. You can do this through a home equity line of credit, also known as a HELOC. A HELOC has characteristics of a mortgage loan and a credit card, so I will briefly discuss this to give you a better understanding. If you fail to pay your mortgage, the bank can take your home because it's a secure loan, meaning your house is the collateral which allows you to have lower interest rates. If you have a credit card, it is considered unsecure and you have much higher interest rates because of it.

A HELOC works similar to a credit card in that you only pay interest on what you owe, and you can access it even after paying it back (just make sure that when you make the final payment, talk to them first and let them know you would like to keep the account open, otherwise it will be closed upon payment). The difference is that your home is the collateral, so your interest rates will be much lower than a conventional loan. A HELOC can cover up to 80 percent of the home's value, so if you have a $200,000 home, you can have an available line of credit for $160,000 for your use. Maybe you have been paying on your house for ten years but have a lot of debt that you want to consolidate. A consolidation loan might have a high interest around 15 percent, but a HELOC can have a significantly lower interest rate (using debt snowball, you can use the money you're saving to pay off the principal amount instead of it going to interest payments with a consolidation loan).

The reason I wanted to talk about HELOCs is because if you are following the methods in this book, you will be paying off half of a homes cost before refinancing and saving for another down payment. If you are debt-free, you can leverage debt by using a HELOC to make a down payment on a property, greatly accelerating the rate at which you grow your real estate portfolio (to use this method, you would use a HELOC initially but then pay it off with a cash-out refinance which will be discussed later). I would like to stress the fact that you need to be very careful doing this because you put in a lot of effort to get out of debt. If you utilize this method, make sure that you are able to easily afford to do so. It is a powerful tool but one I almost didn't put in the book because I don't want people to put themselves in a bad situation. While HELOCs have their place, tools such as a cash-out refinance may be more appropriate.

A cash-out refinance is different than a HELOC in several ways, but that is what makes using them together so amazing. A HELOC has a variable interest rate, and the minimum payments go to interest only. You typically have a ten-year period known as the draw period where you can utilize the line of credit, but afterward, the remaining balance will become your new loan amount (so it's important that you never use your HELOC for something you can't pay back within two years or in six months if you are in your final year of the draw period). A cash-out refinance has a fixed interest rate, and the term is typically made for thirty years (you can request a shorter term) and works similar to a mortgage as you will have a lower-interest rate (usually but not always) and a monthly payment that goes both toward principal and interest. A thing to point out is that a cash-out refinance will have a closing cost while a HELOC has little to no closing cost associated with it. The funds available on HELOCs can be used for a variety of things but should be used strategically on gaining new assets or on the improvement of assets you currently have. Home improvement would be one of those things.

Don't use a HELOC on liabilities or anything that depreciates in value.

Let's say you have a home that is paid off that is valued at $150,000 and you are close to retirement age, but you don't have enough saved up to pay for your retirement. Currently, you are living in your home, but you find out that you could rent it on the market for $1,500 a month ($18,000 before taxes or property manager fees). You need a way to fund your retirement so you decide to get a HELOC loan (it is a great idea to have one opened for any opportunities that may come up) to help you acquire more property (this would give you a $120,000 line of credit). (When applying for a HELOC, if they ask the reason for the HELOC, tell them it's for any opportunities that come up. A great use of a HELOC is for home repairs or additions to the property, such as a new bedroom or bathroom.) You happen to notice several homes listed for the same value of your house in your neighborhood, so you decide to use the HELOC to make a down payment on one of the homes for the purpose of either having it as your primary residence and utilizing house hacking or using it as an investment property and renting it out to a family. Then you get a cash-out refinance to pay off the HELOC and lock in an interest rate. Here is an example of how it can be used.

You ultimately make the choice to rent out your first property with makes $1,350/month after property management fees, and you begin renting out the property you just gained using a HELOC. Even if you put 30 percent down on the home, you didn't have to pay $45,000 of your own income. You utilized your HELOC which was readily available to you by transferring it to your account, and the renters of the new house are paying for the mortgage and leaving you with a few hundred every month in profit. Your first home now has a $45,000 line of credit against it, but it is being paid off by the renters of that home (the money you would typically pay toward interest is now being paid for by the tenants). Your new home is valued at $150,000, but you only owe $105,000 for it. You are essentially using your first property to attain more and without having to use your own income. You are earning more than enough to pay for rent as well as make the payments for the HELOC, but now you will use a cash-out refinance on your first home that you make sure covers the amount to pay off your HELOC in full as well as the closing cost, and paying off your HELOC is the first thing you should do. Now you will have a very low monthly payment spread out over thirty years with fixed interest.

Some people who use this method prefer to let the renters make the minimum payments so they can focus on recycling the method of using a HELOC and cash-out refinance so they can continue acquiring properties. If you like listening to podcasts, you should listen to Bigger Pockets

Podcast who talk about this strategy all the time. While it is definitely viable and highly successful, I don't like being stretched too thin, so I would still recommend paying down the cash-out refinance as quickly as possible and work on paying off half of the balance before refinancing the other property. You won't acquire property as quickly, but you will be in a safer position because of it. I don't like my money going toward interest, and if only the minimum monthly payment is made, you are losing a lot over time which if the amount was instead invested into stocks would grow to hundreds of thousands over the course of thirty years. Even though the tenants are technically paying the interest, if the property is paid off, that difference would instead go to you. If you reinvest that difference, it can equate to hundreds of thousands added to your stock or real estate investments.

Getting back to our example: assuming you used $45,000 of your HELOC, you can get a cash-out refinance to pay off your HELOC, obtain a fixed interest rate, and open up the HELOC in all its glory. Now that you have multiple properties, you can open up a HELOC on all of them. This gives you a lot of leverage that you can utilize for your advantage, but always do your own research and make sure it is a good choice for your current situation.

Even if you are in your fifties, if you have a home with equity, you can easily use it to start increasing your passive income. If you are still working, treat it like any other debt and pay it off as quickly as possible. If you have multiple homes, you can open a HELOC on each one (and if you, for some reason, have credit card debts or other loans and debts, you can use your HELOC like a consolidation loan, except instead of the average 13–18% interest rates on a consolidation loan, and you can get 5–10% from a HELOC. A HELOC doesn't count toward your credit utilization, so by using your HELOC in this manner, you can effectively increase your credit score while lowering your overall interest rates!).

If you decide to use these powerful tools, do so with care and make sure it's sustainable. Build up an emergency fund for each property you have in case something goes wrong. You don't have to use your own money to purchase a home, and if you plan on renting it out, you need to calculate how much of a down payment would place the mortgage payment below what you can rent it for after accounting for fees, taxes, and other expenses. Some people use HELOCs and cash-out refinance to get a new property each year and will sometimes sell a property to make a big payment toward principal on current properties or perhaps invest in a bigger property. I would recommend using it to either obtain more property or to make improvements on the ones you have.

If your home is a three-bedroom with one and a half bath and your home is valued at $150,000, check comparable homes in your neighborhood that are three-bedroom with two and a half bath and see what the value is. It might only cost you 15–30K to have a new bathroom built, but it could increase the value of your home by 40–50K depending on where you live. What you use it for is up to you, but use it responsibly. Don't acquire more debt for the sake of having it. I recommend not having debt at all unless you are using it strategically to generate income.

REAL ESTATE INVESTING THROUGH CROWDFUNDING

If after reading this you decide that you don't want to invest in real estate because you don't want to have to deal with property management, repairs to your home, or if you simply don't believe you will have the time, then real estate investing via crowdfunding can be a great option for you. You can even use crowdfunding to help you save up for a down payment by earning you income through real estate immediately, without actually owning any real estate at all. Crowdfunding is a way for multiple investors to collectively pool their money together for investments that require a lot of capital to get started. This means that you can find crowdfunding deals that you can invest in so you can invest in real estate without ever owning it.

The two main ways to invest in crowdfunding would be through secured loans and equity investments. Secured loans will pay you monthly with a set amount of interest that is low risk (when finding the deals, you will see this information and decide which crowdfunding project you want to invest in) while equity investing works more like the stock market, but instead of owning a portion of the company, you own shares of the property. You get to benefit from the property increasing in value over time as well as for a percentage if the property is sold. How often you get paid depends on the deal you chose, but they are typically paid quarterly.

This is a good way to invest in real estate in a passive manner while your money continues to grow. You can invest in multiple real estate projects and build a rental portfolio that will immediately start earning you passive income. If you continue investing money, you can grow your real estate crowdfunding portfolio until you reach a certain goal and use the money you gained to purchase actual real estate that you will own. Each deal is different, and some have certain time requirements that you have to leave your money invested for. This is so that the person collecting the collected income and investing in properties will be able to have that money to invest. This protects them and the other investors involved and also allows people to invest in real estate with less funds available.

If this is something that interest you, all you have to do is go to a crowdfunding website and register your account. One of the sites that has become more popular because of social media advertisements is a platform called Fundrise, which has a minimum of $500 to invest. While different platforms have different minimums, they also invest in different types of properties. There are also sites like realcrowd.com that has a $25,000 investment as a minimum. I recommend looking at multiple real estate crowdfunding websites/apps and see which one works best for you. Check their reviews or look them up on YouTube and see what people who use those platforms think of it in regard to real estate investing. Between them, it seems that the average return people are getting is around 12 percent. Gaining 12 percent beats the average stock market and lets people grow their wealth while investing in real estate.

Important things to consider when searching for a deal would be how long your investment needs to stay in the account as a minimum and what are the options for withdrawing your investment at a later date. Another thing would be to invest in multiple types of properties. I personally like apartment complexes because in the event of a real estate market crash, people will still need a place to live. Renting an apartment is usually cheaper than renting a home, so there will always be a demand and a safer investment than other real estate types you can find. By investing in several different types of real estate projects using crowdfunding, you are diversifying your real estate portfolio. After the initial deal is set up, you can go online and check to see how your investments are doing. Now all you have to do is decide if you are going to reinvest your earnings into the same property or use it to purchase more projects.

Here is a list of a few different crowdfunding sites for you to get started, but there are many more that I didn't list for you to consider.

- Fundrise.com
- Realcrowd.com
- Realtymogul.com
- Crowdstreet.com
- Patchofland.com

REAL ESTATE INVESTING SUMMARY

If having people sharing your home is not something you want to do, then multifamily homes would be your best option so you still are only required a 3.5 percent down payment with an FHA loan since it will be your primary residence. Remember, this is your future, and you need to do what is right for you. The reason real estate is an important investment for you to make is due to the passive income it can generate and the appreciation of value the property will see over time. My short-term goal with real estate is to generate enough passive income to earn double my expenses. My long-term goal is to make it match my current salary. This will allow me to continue to live how I want to live while being able to use that passive income to reinvest into both real estate and stocks. Long after I'm gone, my children and future grandchildren will be able to live off the things I have built and will be free to live whatever life they choose. I can create generational wealth that can provide for my family and that they can continue to build upon.

You now have two solid ways of getting your own property and being able to live in it for free while generating income from it, and you also can invest in real estate without having to own it at all. You can even use a combination of the single/multifamily homes with crowdfunding so the money you are setting aside to go toward your next property can earn you income while you wait and save. You could even skip purchasing real estate altogether and strictly invest in real estate crowdfunding projects so you can earn money through real estate without having to deal with the properties yourself. There are many ways to invest your income, and I recommend that you look at all the options available to you and figure out which one works the best for you.

With that being said, you also need to have short-term and long-term goals to work toward. Through real estate, you can start earning passive income rather quickly, and by following the same methods in this book, use that increase in your available cash flow to accelerate your plan. Within ten years, there is a great chance you can earn enough passive income to not only cover your expenses but also generate enough passive income to match your current salary. If you continue with this process throughout your life, there is nothing you can't accomplish. Pass on the knowledge you learn to your children and your family. Pass on this knowledge to your church and your circle of friends. Help me by trying to improve the lives of others and end the suffering we see in the world.

If you are married and on the same page financially, working together toward a common goal will accelerate anything you set out to accomplish. Once your budget is established and your debts are paid off, work together with your partner and learn about each other's strengths and weaknesses. As an example, my wife's strengths are my weaknesses and my strengths are her weaknesses. By working together, we are able to pick up where the other is struggling, making us the perfect team.

If you don't have a spouse or partner but have a friend or family member who also wants to make the same journey, work together and you both will accomplish your goals faster. If neither of you have a house and decide to purchase one, you will need to work out the details on how you will go about it. If I were single and doing this plan with a friend, I think the best plan would be to have whoever has the higher credit score purchase the first home (other person has more time to increase theirs) and the other to purchase the second one. If both people save and pay toward the down payment, then both people should do the same with the second property to make it fair. If you choose this route, you will obviously need to trust the person you are doing this with. If I would have known about these methods when I was in high school and utilized them, I have several friends who would have been perfect for this.

FINAL WORDS

I would like to thank each and every one of you who made it this far and can't wait to hear about your journeys. Please leave a review on Amazon to let me know how much this has helped you, how much you were able to reduce your expenses by, how much you were able to increase your income, and how your investments are going! I would love to know the difference it made in your life. You can also email me at jeff.shannon32@yahoo.com so I can be a part of your journey or help with any questions you have along the way. I want to build a community of people who can work together to change the world, and I want you to be a part of it! If you are inspired by what you read, make a YouTube channel and record the progress of your journey. Not only will you build a following, but you will also inspire others to do the same. If you continue recording your journey, you could eventually turn your YouTube channel into another source of income for you!

Thank you for reading this book, and I can't wait to see your results! As promised, I will provide a cheat sheet for those who don't enjoy reading or those who want to use it as a quick reference as well as tips that can save you thousands throughout your life! I hope you enjoy your new life and everything it has to offer. I look forward to hearing from all you future millionaires!

CHEAT SHEETS

Creating your personal financial statement

- It must include all income, expenses, assets, and liabilities.
- If you have a spouse/partner, be on the same page financially.
- Create a new personal financial statement monthly and save your old ones.

Budgeting and reducing expenses

- Again, make sure you and your partner/spouse are on the same page financially.
- Eliminate expenses you don't need.
- Reduce expenses however possible.
- Try to reduce interest rates on anything that has them.
- Call the financial aid departments of hospitals if you have medical bills and negotiate to reduce your monthly payments and see if your income is low enough to qualify for a reduced total amount.

Emergency fund and debt management

- Save six months' worth of your total expenses and put in your savings account.
- Only use emergency fund for emergencies.
- Add your emergency fund to the asset section of your personal financial statement.

- Make sure you make all your minimum monthly payments.
- Use your increased cash flow to pay off your debts using either the avalanche or snowball method.

Budgeting and increasing income

- Ask for a raise and have a sales pitch prepared for your boss to show why you believe you deserve it. Stay polite and professional even if rejected.
- Try to get a secondary job or side hustle.
- If your primary job offers overtime, get as much as you can; 26.7 hours of overtime is worth 40 hours of regular pay.
- Use house hacking methods to generate income with your property.
- You can rent extra space in your home as storage using certain apps.
- Use your vehicle to generate income.
- Drive for services like Uber, Uber Eats, DoorDash, Grubhub, and Lyft for additional income and a flexible schedule.
- Consider getting paid for having advertisements on your vehicle.
- Use apps for finding side hustles and side gigs.
- Consider relocating to an area with higher pay and lower cost of living.
- Create a general résumé and know how to make targeted résumés to send to companies you want to work for.
- Know how to prepare for a job interview, research the company, and how to dress professionally.
- There are better alternatives than just college.

Increasing your credit score

- Make all payments on time.
- Don't use more than 30 percent of your total available credit limit.

- Keep credit card accounts open even if you don't use them.
- Know that having different kinds of debt is actually good for your credit score.
- Don't apply for multiple credit cards within a short time frame.
- Dispute all negative items on your credit reports.

Investing in stocks

- Use dollar-cost averaging by investing the same amount, every month.
- Know that investing 1K per month for twenty-four years with an average annual growth of 10 percent will make you a millionaire.
- Accelerate the benefits of dollar-cost averaging by investing funds you that you will set aside each month into your portfolio during times when the stock drops in value which will buy you more shares than it would otherwise.
- Invest using low-cost index funds and ETFs for lower fees and more diversity in your portfolio if you are new to investing. Invest in individual companies once you become more familiar with identifying high-quality companies.
- Proper asset allocation diversifies your portfolio and helps to protect your investments. Invest in different industries and asset classes.
- Rebalance your portfolio whenever needed to return it back to your predetermined ratio.
- Automate investing by using apps to simplify the experience and take the stress and emotions out of investing.
- Invest in real estate (single-family homes).
- Find and purchase a home with three to four bedrooms and preferably two bathrooms.
- Live in one room and rent out the others using the house hacking methods mentioned in the book.
- Use the income from the house hacking to pay the monthly mortgage payment.

- A week or two after the mortgage payment, call the lender and ask to make a payment toward principal only (and use your available cash flow to pay as much as you can).
- Once mortgage is halfway paid off, refinance and look for another property.
- Repeat all steps above for the new property and list the first home to rent through a property manager.
- Use income from house hacking on the second property to pay the monthly mortgage payment, and you use your available cash flow to pay off the first property.
- Once first property is paid off, save for a down payment and find another property to use as a rental and rent it through a property manager.
- Use the income from the rental to pay the mortgage monthly payment and use your income to pay off your second mortgage. Then you can continue this process to accumulate real estate and passive income.
- While doing so, try to keep the total of all mortgages below 25 percent of your total income to provide you a safety net.
- Have an emergency fund for each property set aside, preferably in an account that your property manager has access to for emergencies.
- If you consider using leverage to increase your real estate portfolio, make sure you aren't spread too thin (over-leveraged).

Investing in real estate (multifamily)

- Invest in a multifamily property, live in one unit as your primary residence, and rent out the other units for generating income.
- You can still use the house hacking methods in the unit you are living in, just make sure there is enough parking for each unit and any roommates you get.
- Use a property manager for the other units to make the process as easy on you as possible.

- Location and parking spaces for each unit is an important thing to consider.
- Use the same strategy of paying off half of the mortgage, refinancing, and purchasing another multifamily home. Live in one of the units as your permanent residence to still qualify for the 3.5 percent FHA down payment.
- Save up an emergency fund for each multifamily property and keep it in an account that the property manager has access to in case of an emergency in the units.
- If you consider using leverage to increase your real estate portfolio, make sure you aren't spread too thin (over-leveraged).

Investing in real estate through crowdfunding

- Real estate investing through crowdfunding is a way to invest in real estate without actually owning or managing the properties.
- Secured loans investing makes you the bank, earning a fixed amount of interest and payments over a fixed amount of time that is paid to you monthly by the investor.
- Equity investing is similar to stocks as you hold "shares" or a portion of the property and see gains through regular payments and price appreciation of the property. You also earn income if the property is sold.
- Equity investment payments vary and depend on each specific deal but most pay quarterly.
- Invest in different types of real estate to diversify your portfolio.
- There are many crowdfunding sites to choose from, but some of the popular ones are fundrise.com, realcrowd.com, realtymogul.com, crowdstreet.com, and patchofland.com.
- Average returns through real estate crowdfunding are 12 percent annual average.

WAYS TO SAVE MONEY

When purchasing a vehicle, you can save a lot of money by buying a vehicle that is at least five years old **(in five years, they lose at least 70 percent of their value)** while still being covered under the warranty and in good condition. A formula created by the IRS that companies use to determine the depreciation of a vehicle is the *straight-line depreciation method.* You take the current value of the new vehicle and subtract the estimated value of the same type of vehicle that is around five years old and then divide that number by five. As an example, let's say the new cost of the vehicle is $32,000 and a used one that is six years older **(the closer to five, the better)** cost $7,680.

It is $32,000 - $7,680 = $24,320, so $24,320 divided by six years is equal to $4,053.33. This means that type of vehicle lost $4,053.33 in value every year. If you purchased the used vehicle for $7,680 and you paid for it in cash **(no money lost to interest and no monthly vehicle payments)**, the value would depreciate at a much slower rate and allow you to invest all the income you would be spending on monthly payments and interest. That $24,320 you save, if invested and left alone at an average annual income of 10.5 percent, would be worth $66,006.45 in ten years and $179,146.83 in twenty years.

When it comes to electronics, they can come with extremely high prices. To save you some money, consider purchasing used or refurbished electronics. There is an app called Back Market that sells electronics that have been sent back to the companies and refurbished, and they also come with warranties and warranty information for significantly less than brand-new. They have anything from headphones, to gaming systems, to computers. You can save several hundred to several thousand on high quality electronics for bargain prices.

When it comes to reducing your expenses, one of the easier ways you can do so is by cooking at home. While cooking at home will save you a lot of money, cooking at home *and* meal prepping can save you both time and money. There are a few appliances that make this process easier, and that would be a slow cooker and a deep freezer **(if you have space)**. Simply prep your meals in advance and put them in your deep freezer for a later date. The day before the meal would be eaten, place it in the refrigerator so it will thaw out by the next day. This can save you hundreds every month, which compounded over time can save you hundreds of thousands of dollars.

If you want to get some of the certifications mentioned earlier in this book, there several ways to do so. You obviously have to take a test and pass to be certified, but the time frame and how you study can be very different. You can take boot camps, such as "Security + Bootcamps" which are normally two-week classes where every day you will take a practice test and study the material, and after doing this for two weeks, you will take the real exam. They have a high pass rate, plus you get hands-on experience while also reading the material. It's probably the best option to get the certification plus the experience, but it usually comes with a cost around five thousand dollars. While that cost may seem to be too high, it's significantly less time and money than a college degree, and the average income from holding that certification is higher than a majority of degrees anyway.

If you want to study the certification but don't want to take the "boot camp," you can go to a website like itpro.tv and pay the monthly or annual subscription to get access to all study material, labs **(if you pay a few hundred extra a year for the premium)**, practice exams, and other things for practically every certification out there. You can pay the annual price once and then study for and get certified for as many certifications as you want. You still have to pay to take the exams, but this website is one of the best when it comes to studying for the test. The last and cheapest options would be purchasing the books, which cost around thirty dollars and have everything you need in book form to study although you will still need to pay to take your exam.

If you are paying a mortgage, know that only paying the minimum will result in you paying somewhere around 2.5 times the cost of the mortgage **(a $200,000 home at 5 percent interest with a thirty-year loan results in you actually paying $386,511.57)**. By making additional payments every month, you can have the house easily paid off in less than ten years by paying additional payments toward principal every month. Go online and search for loan amortization calculator or download a loan amortization calculator app. If it has an option for making additional monthly payments toward principal, play with the numbers of what you can afford to pay and see how soon you can pay it off.

Most homes have to constantly run their air conditioner or eater, and this is due to many factors. Windows are a big source of this problem as heat coming in through the windows tend to become magnified during the summer, and you lose a lot of heat through those same windows during the winter. A cheap option is to buy window blinds specifically made to combat this issue or the curtains which do the same thing. You can find them online or in many stores, but adding these to your windows can save you thousands every year. This can greatly reduce the amount of electricity you use each month.

If you already know what you consider your dream job to be but don't have the requirements yet, find and print the job description for that specific job and highlight the requirements they have and the qualifications they desire. Now you want to find jobs that allow you to get the experience and skills that are relevant for your dream position. This allows you to have a relevant job history on your résumé, experience in your desired field, and increases the chance of getting your dream job. Once you have all the requirements, make a targeted résumé for that company or pay to have one made for you.

This will ultimately allow you to advance your career as you go while gaining experience that will make you an asset for the company who hires you. Every job you take before that should have some skill or experience that would be relevant for your dream position. This is a long-term method that increases your chances of success. Do it while also obtaining the necessary certifications or degrees needed.

Use credit cards once you are debt-free instead of a debit card, but make sure you pay off the full balance before the end of the billing cycle. Use a credit card with rewards that fit your needs. Many credit cards don't have an annual fee, but the ones that do tend to come with better rewards that may or may not be a better option for you. Look at all the rewards before making your decision. One of the main rewards include points obtained through every purchase you make, with certain purchases earning more points than others.

This is an easy way to get an extra thousand a year in free cash, or you can use it to get free flights and hotels. There are so many different rewards available; spend some time going through to decide which is better for you. I travel frequently and found that the American Express Gold offers better rewards than most credit cards, and I actively use the majority of the ones they have. Although I pay an annual fee, the rewards I get are worth it. You are essentially getting paid to improve your credit score!

If you want to go to college but don't want to accumulate a lot of student debt, there are a few options you can utilize. One is to download an app called Scholly, and after entering your personal information, it will show you every scholarship you meet the requirements for. Another option is to talk to colleges in your area that you are interested in and ask about job opportunities available. Some colleges will allow certain employees and their family members to attend for free or at reduced prices. I don't know how many colleges offer this, but I know several that have in the past, so I'm sure there are a lot more.

ABOUT THE AUTHOR

Jeff Shannon, a distinguished twelve-year US Navy submarine veteran, brings a unique blend of military discipline and advanced electronics and engineering systems education to his endeavors. Post-military service, he charted an inspiring path of self-improvement, immersing himself in finance and business management. Fueled by an unwavering commitment to bettering his family's financial future, Mr. Shannon's tenacity and new-found expertise empowered him to eliminate over $100,000 in debt within a mere 1.5 years, simultaneously witnessing a remarkable tripling of his income.

A testament to the transformative power of knowledge, hard work, and dedication, Jeff Shannon is not just an author but a living example of financial resilience. He believes that the insights encapsulated within this book possess the potential to positively impact the lives of individuals striving to enhance their financial circumstances. With a passion for sharing the wealth of wisdom he has accumulated, Mr. Shannon endeavors to guide and inspire readers on their transformative journeys.